"This book was written with the scientific zeal of a gerontologist, the spiritual concern of a theologian and yet the emotion and practical attention of a daughter who had to face that most difficult decision herself. This presentation should be at the top of our list when considering our own stance."

WALTER T. LINN, Ph.D.
Christian Family Sociologist
Director, Genesis Counseling Services

"If you're looking for a stimulating book, then read this book. In her solid style Dorothea Nyberg offers insights that will stir your imagination and challenge your convictions. Tough questions — honest answers. Read this book for the sake of your family and yourself."

DENNIS RAINEY, National Director
Family Ministry
Campus Crusade for Christ International

Life Support

Dorothea Marvin Nyberg

Here's Life Publishers

First Printing, April 1988

Published by
HERE'S LIFE PUBLISHERS, INC.
P.O. Box 1576
San Bernardino, CA 92402

HLP Product No. 952051
© 1988, Dorothea Marvin Nyberg
All rights reserved.
Printed in the United States of America.

Library of Congress Cataloging-in-Publication Data
    Nyberg, Dorothea M. (Dorothea Marvin), 1923-
      Life Support
      Includes bibliographical references.
      1. Church work with the terminally ill. 2. Right to die — Religious
    aspects — Christianity. I. Title.
    BV4460.6.N83   1988   241'.6424   87-19749
    ISBN 0-89840-203-4 (pbk.)

Scripture quotations designated TLB are from *The Living Bible,* © 1971 by
Tyndale House Publishers, Wheaton, Illinois.
Scripture quotations designated NIV are from *The Holy Bible, New International
Version,* © 1978 by New York International Bible Society, published by
the Zondervan Corporation, Grand Rapids, Michigan.
Scripture quotations designated KJV are from the *King James Version* of the
Bible.
Scripture quotations designated RSV are from *The Revised Standard Version,*
© 1962 by The World Publishing Company, New York, New York.

Portions of chapter 1 of this book appeared previously as an article in *Family
Life Today,* April 1984, pages 38-39.

For More Information, Write:
    L.I.F.E. — P.O. Box A399, Sydney South 2000, Australia
    Campus Crusade for Christ — Box 300, Vancouver, B.C. V6C 2X3, Canada
    Campus Crusade for Christ — Pearl Assurance House, 4 Temple Row, Birmingham, B2 5HG, England
    Lay Institute for Evangelism — P.O. Box 8786, Auckland 3, New Zealand
    Campus Crusade for Christ — P.O. Box 240, Colombo Court Post Office, Singapore 9117
    Great Commission Movement of Nigeria — P.O. Box 500, Jos, Plateau State Nigeria, West Africa
    Campus Crusade for Christ International — Arrowhead Springs, San Bernardino, CA 92414, U.S.A.

Contents

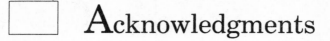Acknowledgments

*To my mother and father, whose deaths
taught me to confront loss and to have
compassion for those who face the trauma
of having to make life-or-death decisions
. . . with a prayer that the experiences
shared in this book will help others who
must travel the same road.*

Thanks to my friend and mentor, Kay Murrin,
who read and reread the manuscript
and who kept me in line
and encouraged me through the painful parts.

And blessings to my husband and best friend, Don,
who suffered from neglect
and put up with a wife turned author.

TABOO

We are not ready
to talk about death.
We say we would rather
wait until spring.
Death is a subject
for discreet distances.
It is someone else's
destiny —
not ours —
and preferably never.
We are afraid
to touch its skin
and test for chill.
We are afraid.
We are afraid.
We are afraid.

Thomas John Carlisle

*Finding peace about a hard
decision*

1 | We
Faced the Dilemma

> *For this great God is our God forever and ever. He will be
> our guide until we die (Psalm 48:14, TLB).*

THE SIREN SCREAM heralded the help we needed.
Waiting for the paramedics was not new to me, but
memories of previous incidents were of no comfort.

On too many other occasions I'd also found Mom unconscious, unable to call me. Paramedics came this time,
too, with their skills and compassion, and carefully dis-
patched her to the hospital.

When she regained consciousness and was able to talk,
she scolded me. "Dorothea, I told you the last time this happened to go out in the kitchen and do your dishes or bake
a cake — anything, but don't call the paramedics. They only
haul me back here to the hospital where they build me up
again for a few months. I want to be released from this
merry-go-round. I pray to go to heaven to be with Dad."
Then with a twinkle in her near-blind eyes she continued,
"Maybe the reason it's taking so long is I guess I want to
see Dad more than Jesus. Is that terrible?"

"No," I reassured her. "I'm certain God is delighted
with such a strong and lasting love. He understands."

We'd been through this procedure many times. Mom

had her first stroke a few months after Dad's death. We transformed our home into a convalescent hospital and prayed that we would be able to care for her until the Lord chose to take her home.

We worked through therapy sessions, and we laughed about other situations. Once, when she could still hobble with my support, a small boy asked his mother in a shrill voice, "Mommy, babies can't walk, but she's an old lady. Why can't she walk?"

At each hospitalization, when she could swallow again and the intravenous feeding was discontinued, she was released to return home. We'd begin working with liquids and then move to strained food, to chopped food, and finally back to a normal diet. Each episode left her with more paralysis and less ability to help with her personal needs, but we struggled and made laughter a part of our lives.

Decision Time

The last time this happened, two days before our youngest son's wedding, Mom's speech slurred. She began having trouble swallowing and her temperature started climbing. The doctor quickly advised, "Call an ambulance and get her to the hospital. She must be dehydrating."

The week following the wedding my husband Don underwent retina repair surgery while Mom was still in the hospital. During Don's recovery, our eldest son David, who was visiting at the time, took me aside and said, "Mom, Donny and I have been talking about you and Dad. The only time you get away is when Aunt Peg comes to stay with Grandma. When Donny lived at home you went out for dinner now and then, but he's married now and that situation has changed. It's been four years since Dad has had a full-time wife. His surgery wasn't simple and neither of you are kids anymore. You must put Grandma in a convalescent hospital. Think about it, please."

David was asking me to think about the unthinkable — putting my mother into a situation that seemed unbearable to me. At first I refused to consider David's suggestion, but as the days wore on, I realized I had to consider this unhappy alternative. Don's recovery was taking longer than we had anticipated. We told Mom we couldn't bring her home because I could not take care of two patients. She understood, but expressed her hope that it would not be permanent.

What made Mom's stay in the convalescent hospital even more difficult for me was that her care was not satisfactory. She was incontinent as a result of this last stroke and many times when I arrived at the nursing home to feed her, I'd find her lying in a wet bed. Her mind was alert and she told the nurses that she was wet, but the aides were negligent in caring for her.

One such day I called my sister in tears to report the continuing problem. "Peg, I know I can't care for Mom at home, but this is intolerable. What can we do?"

"Let me investigate a convalescent hospital here," she replied. "A friend of mine had her father in this one for several years and he had excellent care. I'll call you tomorrow. Hang in there!"

When I went back to see Mom that evening I told her about my call. "If Peg can get you into a good hospital in Santa Fe, do you want to go?"

"If I can't go home with you," she smiled woefully, "anything will be better than this."

The next day Peg reported, "This facility looks excellent. They have a vacancy they'll hold for four days, but do you think you can get her here?"

"We'll make it somehow," I assured her, and sent up a quick prayer from my heart for the needed help from the Lord. We left on an early morning flight, and landed safely with little trauma.

It hurt to say goodbye, but I returned to California knowing we'd made the best of an unhappy situation.

Several months later Peg called me. She was crying. "Dorothea, Mom is semi-conscious and they don't know what's the matter. They want to transfer her to the acute-care hospital. I told them no." I felt her pain across the miles. "Did I do the right thing?" she asked.

I was silent, held my breath and prayed for the wisdom to know God's will.

"Are you still there?" Peg asked. "Did you hear my question?"

"Wait a minute, I need to collect my thoughts." I had faced this situation so many times while Mom lived with us. The answer then was to call the paramedics. I couldn't just stand by and watch or wait for her to die; now the situation differed. She was in a convalescent hospital, a good one, with round-the-clock nursing care and someone who would be there if she needed help. Was this the time to allow God to take her home? Was it time to say, "No more heroic measures"? I could hear Mom's voice say, "This is what I want!"

As these thoughts ran through my mind, a feeling of peace enveloped me, a sensation of being in perfect tune with God's will.

"Yes!" My reply to my sister was emphatic. "Remember, Mom told the doctor when I brought her there that no life support was to be used. You heard her." I tried to keep my voice calm and hide my churning emotions. "Why does he talk acute-care hospital now?"

"Her doctor is out of town. The one who came doesn't know her or anything about her."

I knew what my sister was facing. I'd been through it many times. Doubt crept in again. Should we okay another session in a primary hospital with more I.V.s?

Peace

Closing my eyes, I prayed for and again received the promised peace. I took a deep breath and continued, "Peg, call the hospital and tell them you've talked to me and that I agree with you 100 percent. Remind them that Mom told the doctor she didn't want any life support. This is following her wishes."

It was a tough decision. *Are we playing God?* I questioned, but from deep within me came the conviction that this was the right thing to do. Christmas was just a few weeks away, and I could visualize the happiness of Mom and Dad celebrating Jesus' birthday with Him.

The nursing staff turned her every hour, from side to back and back to side, and kept her mouth moistened with water. She never regained consciousness, and two days later, on December first, Mom died.

Her memorial service was held in the chapel of our church. A dear pastor friend who had served the church of my childhood in Minnesota officiated as she had requested. "We are here today," Dr. Bailey began, "for a celebration. A celebration of Margaret Marvin's entrance into heaven, where a giant jubilee is in progress. She is with all her friends and loved ones who have gone before."

I squeezed Don's hand and smiled at my sister and our children. Yes, we had made the correct decision. Mom at eighty-nine had the right to be released from this life. Her death had become a celebration!

In the Lord's Hands

June, a dear friend of mine, also experienced a decision-making time with her elderly mother. Her parents had just celebrated their 50th wedding anniversary, but shortly thereafter her mother had to be institutionalized because she was unable mentally to cope with the routines of life. During her mother's hospitalization her father suffered a severe heart attack and died.

According to June, his death was a blessing in many ways. Separation from his wife had been difficult for her father, whereas her mother simply didn't understand. Her mother's psychiatrist advised a full wake and funeral service so she would accept the reality of her husband's death. This was accomplished and with treatment she improved enough to be able to move to a retirement home that provided twenty-four-hour care. Because she could not accept the fact that she was a diabetic and also had high blood pressure and glaucoma, she required a controlled environmental situation.

When June's mother's physical condition worsened several weeks before her 75th birthday, she was hospitalized again. June felt fortunate that the hospital consulted her before beginning *extraordinary* treatment. This is one of the advantages of a small-town hospital where the family is known personally. June and her sisters cried and prayed, searched the Scriptures, then cried and prayed some more. They talked with their husbands and pastors, then met again with the attending physicians. The decision was made to leave their mother in the Lord's hands, and not hold on to her for more pain and suffering. She was kept comfortable and they sat at her bedside, held her hand and felt that last tremor as she was released to what they knew would be a happier life.

June emphasizes the fact that they have never regretted their decision.

Due to the advances in medical technology, each generation is living longer as well as expanding in numbers. Thus more families will be forced to make these tough decisions. It is not a happy process, but with the help of the Lord, Scripture, friends and family, decisions can be reached that will bring peace to all concerned.

2 Tough Questions

> *I weep with grief; my heart is heavy with sorrow;*
> *encourage and cheer me with your words*
> (Psalm 119:28, TLB).

- TO ALLOW OR to cause a person's death — is there a difference?
- Is the doctor's responsibility to prolong life more important than his responsibility to relieve suffering?

In this chapter we are asking the questions that are normally asked, even by Christians, and it is important that we help families resolve them from a biblical perspective.

Playing God

- What about the will of God?
- When forced into the decision-making position, are we playing God?

The Christian Action Council states, "The notion of man determining the point of his own death and then the point at which others should die is predominant over the notion of God as the sovereign over death."[1] However, two questions conflict with this statement:

- Is God sovereign over death today?
- Or — because He allowed us the freedom of

choice—have the medical miracle machines, medications and doctors become the final authorities?

One Form of Love

Allowing a loved one to die without being "hooked up" to life-support systems is one form of love, although that point will be argued by some. It was because our family loved our mother that we were willing to fight for her right to die. At the end, when comatose, Mom was unable to speak for herself but she had previously requested no life support. In her estimation she was not living, only existing. With no fear of death, and with a strong love for her Lord and her husband, she wanted to be with both in heaven. We felt it our Christian duty to refuse treatment and allow God to release her from her existence as our blind, diapered and partially paralyzed mother.

First Samuel comforted me with the Lord's assurance: "I don't make decisions the way you do! Men judge by outward appearance, but I look at a man's thoughts and intentions" (1 Samuel 16:7b, TLB).

The book of Job helped, too, by telling me that in death the weary are set free. And Mom *was* tired. She trusted the Lord, knowing that with Him all would be well. God knew our decision was made for the right reason.

Living or Dying?

Most people want to avoid the subject of "dying." Voices become hushed and laughter forgotten when death arrives on the doorstep. In contrast, our society admires and idolizes youthful, healthy, vigorous people. Yet we cannot ignore dying: Death is as natural as birth, and it enters every family circle.

As medical science continues to develop new technologies to sustain the functions of failing organs, more families will face life-or-death decisions. The use of life-support systems extends the interval between living and dying. The dilemma then focuses on the questions:

- Are we prolonging life or are we prolonging death?
- How do we differentiate between the two?
- Would a merciful God condemn a person to months or years of pain and suffering?

Medical institutions feed patients who are in the final stages of life when feeding will not save their lives but only prolong the act of dying. In the past, patients were pronounced dead when neither heartbeat nor breathing was detected. Now that medicine and machines are more sophisticated, the dying are kept living longer.

To understand this ability of medicine to keep vegetative bodies alive, we must realize that the human brain has two sections, the cortex and the stem. The cortex controls one's thinking and moving, and the brain stem controls respiratory and circulatory systems. When the brain stem dies at the same time as the cortex, the patient will expire unless life-support systems are set in motion. It is possible, however, for the cortex to die while the brain stem remains alive. When that happens the patient enters a chronic vegetative state in which the respiration and circulation can function as long as the body is provided with fluids, nutrition, medication and routine care. Thus, distinguishing between life and death becomes complicated.

No Easy Answers

- What about quality of life?
- Who decides *what quality* of life should be acceptable for *what person*?
- Should consideration be given to the cost of the development of these new medical marvels?
- Is the "heroic," mechanical prolonging of the life of an incurable patient sensible if it might bankrupt the family or if the excessive amount of money expended could have saved many other lives?

These questions incorporate facts that need to be discussed in the light of biblical information, and we will look at them in later chapters.

Euthanasia

The dictionary describes euthanasia as the painless putting to death of persons suffering from incurable diseases.

I want to make it clear that I do not endorse the process described above. This discussion is intended merely to help you distinguish between the two extremes: (1) actually hastening a death; and (2) endlessly prolonging the dying.

Euthanasia is not a new subject. In the United States, the first bill attempting its regulation was introduced in the Ohio Legislature in 1906. That bill would have legalized voluntary euthanasia for adults of sound mind who are fatally hurt, terminally ill, or suffering extreme pain. The bill was sent to a committee for study, but it never passed.

"In 1912 a woman petitioned the New York State Legislature to permit her physician to put her painlessly to death because she was suffering from an incurable disease and was in constant pain."[2] She failed to secure legal sanctions.

- Is it morally or legally right to keep a vegetative body alive?

Another case made headlines in the newspapers and on television. The Karen Quinlan case in 1976 became the first one in which the court decision allowed hospital personnel to take a brain-dead person off a respirator. At that time it was believed her death would be imminent if the respirator was removed.

At her parent's request, however, high-nutrient feedings and antibiotics for recurring infections were continued and she lived — to exist in a chronic vegetative state, unable to communicate with anyone (a testimony to the uncertainty in life-and-death assessments of patients).

Her death in 1985, nine years after the respirator was turned off, proved that the estimated 10,000 other such patients in permanent comas can live an indeterminate length of time with the aid of artificial nutrition and hydration.

In later court cases the legality of withholding nutri-

tional support and fluids administered by nasogastric or intravenous tubes has been questioned. In 1981 two
California physicians were charged with murder for
withdrawing such support from an irreversibly comatose
patient even though the act had been performed at the request of the family. The physicians were absolved of the
charges but undoubtedly it made many doctors less willing
to follow like requests.

Dying With Dignity

- Do patients have the right to choose to die with
  dignity?
- Is it morally or legally right to allow patients to
  starve to death?

Elizabeth Bouvia, a severe cerebral palsy patient, is a
quadriplegic with degenerative crippling arthritis. She is in
extreme pain and seems doomed in her struggle to find
relief from her suffering. Her case was sensationalized by
the news media in 1983 when she refused to eat and her
weight dropped drastically. The health care provider would
not allow her to starve herself and inserted a feeding tube.
Elizabeth Bouvia sued and lost the case.

In 1986, when Bouvia was no longer able to swallow or
tolerate the feeding tube, she appealed her case and lost.
The court claimed that if the feeding tube was removed it
would shorten her life. During this period her condition had
deteriorated. Lying flat on her back, totally dependent on
others, she could move some fingers on one hand, had par-
tial use of facial muscles and the ability to move her head.
She is an intelligent young woman who wanted to starve
herself because she felt she had no other choice.

Patient's Rights

- Can a patient be certain of tender loving care at
  home or in a care facility *if* he or she chooses to
  endure the suffering?

Continually, more and more facts come to light about
the poor care in many of these places. Not all facilities are
bad, but there should be *no* bad ones. Senior citizens and

disabled people deserve the best TLC possible.

There are other considerations as well.

- If patients are incompetent, who should make decisions for them?
- What if the surrogate has different values from those of the patient?

Medical technology has made giant strides, but laws regarding death and dying as well as ethical judgments lag far behind and the result is the life-support dilemma. Courts across the country are still being petitioned about the rights of the patient or his surrogate to make life-and-death decisions.

- Do patients really know what they want when they beg to be allowed to die?

Consider the case of a sixty-six-year-old diabetic woman who had one leg removed because of a loss of circulation. Later her remaining leg became infected and gangrene sent poison throughout her body. Given the diagnosis, and told that the treatment required removal of the leg to save her life, she said, "No! Never!"

During the next two days her doctor badgered her until she relented. Her remaining leg was removed. She lay in ICU with tubes running fluids, antibiotics and nutrition into her veins. A respirator was connected to her lungs by a tube in her windpipe. When her doctor entered the room, she motioned him to come near, put her arms around him and gave him a kiss. Then she wrote on a piece of paper, "Thank you for not letting me die!"

Suicide

On the other side of the dilemma, in some instances death is put in a holding pattern in the belief that it is for the benefit of the patient. This situation is described in *The Woman Said Yes,* by Jessamyn West. She discusses her sister's cancer with the doctor:

"How long does she have?"
"I don't know. Organically nothing is wrong with her. At the moment she just has this mechanical obstruction.

It is painful. Without the enemas, she could not live. The tumor will grow. Will rip and tear. It is like a cannon ball working its way through her. Eventually, she will bleed and fester and putrefy."

"She will not wait for that."

[The doctor] said once more, "That is what many people believe at this stage."[3]

Later the book tells how Jessamyn helped her sister commit suicide.

- Did her sister have the right to do that?
- Was it fair of her to ask for Jessamyn's help?
- What obligation does the law have in a case like this?

In order to face the suffering of a loved one and handle the tough decisions involved, we need a network of resources.

- Do our churches provide areas of strength for suffering patients and their families?
- Could our churches act as monitoring agencies for care facilities?
- What obligation does the church or religion have?

Churches should be caring communities, able to reach out to their members and the world at large in times of need. They should be able to help with these questions that have no definite answers.

Tough Decisions

These are all tough questions especially from the Christian perspective, and many families are being forced to face them because of the wonders medical science is developing.

We faced that dilemma with my mother, and the decision was not easy. Our choice was made several years ago, and we have felt nothing but peace since that time. However, our decision—although correct for us—might not be proper for another family caught in their own life-or-death situation.

3 | Opponents and Proponents

I am the resurrection and the life. He who believes in me will live, even though he dies; and whoever lives and believes in me will never die. Do you believe this?
(John 11:25,26, NIV)

THE APOSTLE PAUL said, "The greatest of these [spiritual attributes] is love" (1 Corinthians 13:13). It is *love* that allows us to sanction life-support systems and it is *love* that allows us to say no to them. There is no set rule to follow. Each individual must face the problem when and if decision time enters his life.

It would be easier if choices did not have to be made, but that conclusion has a bad connotation. We never want to lose our freedom to make decisions. In his novel, *Winterflight,* the late Joseph Bayly depicts the other side of the spectrum. A family of the future is faced with a devastating problem. Their son is a hemophiliac; born at home, his condition had not been discovered by the authorities. When he fell off his bike and bruised his hip (a serious injury for a hemophiliac) his parents had nowhere to turn for medical help. If authorities learned of the child's condition he would be sent to the Organ Factory.

In the time period of the novel, only "perfect" humans were allowed life. The grandfather in the story had reached

22

the age of seventy-five and received his notice to report to the "thanotel" for termination.[1]

Of course, this is only a novel. If a novel had been written years ago, though, about a future super race, about a man such as Hitler, would anyone have believed it could ever become a realization?

We certainly hope our nation will never be as godless as the United States in Bayly's novel, yet one must consider such a possibility before the freedom to disconnect any life-support system is legally and freely given.

Drawing the Line

In 1957 Pope Pius XII made public a statement that man has a duty to preserve life and health, but is obliged to use only ordinary methods to achieve this end — those which do not impose ponderous hardships on the patient or others. Although spoken years ago, this addresses the dilemmas posed by today's health questions. Where does one draw the line in life-and-death situations?

In *Mother's Song,* John Sherrill writes of his mother's last illness, and relates this disturbing fact:

> Sitting in silence by Mother's bedside, I allowed something to surface which my conscious mind had been avoiding.
> Mother had little fear of death, but she did fear a bad dying. Like most of us she dreaded the idea of being incapacitated, and then being hooked up to machines, put on chemicals, fed intravenously and kept alive artificially.[2]

Sherrill had flown home from Hong Kong because of an uncanny feeling. When he arrived in the States he discovered his mother had been hospitalized. She was in bed, her arms tied to the bed rails. Plastic tubes ran between the bottles and her arms — exactly what she had been adamantly against.

He tells of talking to the doctor, and fearing the doctor's reaction to a request to remove the I.V.s, but the doctor raised none. Then came the same questions my sister and I had asked each other. We, too, knew our mother's desires just as John Sherrill knew his mother's wishes, but we still pondered the question of what God wanted. Had medical technology not made such dramatic progress, both of our mothers would have died quietly without our intervention, as June's mother did.

After watching his mother struggle against her restraints, Sherrill discussed the situation with members of his family and they agreed to the removal of the I.V.s. His mother's composure then became one of perfect peace. He spent hours reading to her from the psalms. Each time he read, her eyes opened but seemed sightless. As Sherrill left the hospital and walked to his car one day a realization came:

> I knew at last what it was. Mother's eyes were the eyes of a baby. You can't get in touch with a baby's mind, but you never doubt his awareness; and so it was with Mother.
> The baby is coming from God; Mother was going to God. And both conveyed to me that same whisper of eternity.[3]

While love prompts some people to sustain the life of a loved one as long as possible, it also allows removal of the bottles and hoses and respirators and letting death come naturally. For our family it was not a medical or legal decision. After much prayer, and knowing our mother's relationship with the Lord, our decision was based on our understanding of biblical principles and simply the fact that we loved our mother and wanted what she wanted — to be released from her useless earthly body.

The Hemlock Society

One group that has settled on some conclusions in these matters is the Hemlock society. While I do not necessarily endorse their conclusions, I do need to tell you about them. You will encounter these philosophies in your reading, on the media, and as you talk with various people, and you need to understand their implications.

In my research I discovered that, unlike many people's concept of the group, they do not promote suicide per se.

Their aim is to help the terminally ill person who suffers beyond his or her capability. The questions then become:

- What is the definition of capability?
- And who should determine how much a person can handle?

Some people have a higher threshold for pain than others.

Here are some quotes from Derek Humphrey's book, *Let Me Die Before I Wake*, regarding some of these theories:

Although the case for voluntary euthanasia has been discussed by philosophers for centuries, the excesses of modern medicine are only just beginning to bring the argument to the wider public consciousness.[4]

Suicide for an emotional reason is always tragic, and almost always unnecessary.[5]

Modern medicine does much to prolong lives, but the extension of life does not necessarily mean that it has extended its quality.[6]

We believe that the preparation for dying involves more complex problems than the mere act of deliberately ending one's life.[7]

Everyone wishes to die well. Quickly, without pain, without anguish, and sparing loved ones a protracted deathbed watch. Quite often this manner of death comes naturally from sudden heart failure or from collapse leading to a coma followed by a rapid end. But not always. The only way to be reasonably certain of a good death is to plan it, and plan if at all possible, when one is still in good health.[8]

The Hemlock Society, an educational organization, supports the option of active voluntary euthanasia (self-deliverance) for the advanced terminally ill mature adult, or the seriously incurable, physically ill person.[9]

John Jefferson Davis, in reviewing another Humphrey book for *Eternity* magazine, says that the author believes laws prohibiting suicide and mercy killing should be canceled. Davis points out though, that the sixth commandment, "Thou shalt not kill," prevents us from accepting suicide or mercy killings. "The legalization of 'voluntary' and 'requested' mercy killing could open floodgates to the *involuntary* killing of the senile, the handicapped newborn, and other categories of 'burdensome' and 'useless' human beings."[10]

Euthanasia is a particularly controversial subject, and the arguments for or against it must be approached with extreme caution. One priest said, "Don't call it euthanasia when it is simply removing medical intervention."

Most decisions about when to hook up a patient to life support, or whether to keep him on it, have been made by hospital administrators, doctors, insurance companies and the government. These issues necessitated the creation of "bioethic committees," now a part of many hospital staffs.

Bioethics is the study of the moral and social implications of practices and developments in medicine and the life sciences. The decisions that have to be made cover not only medical, but also ethical, legal, moral, religious and financial dimensions.

In Orange County, California, an organization has been developed through the joint efforts of Ellen Severoni of the Orange County Health Planning Council, and Sister Corrine Bayley, director of the Center for Bioethics, St. Joseph Health System. Along with a multitude of other interested people they work under the banner of California Health Decisions. The group raises questions such as:

- Is it appropriate in every case to use life-prolonging technology?
- Do people have the right to health care on an equal basis?
- What areas of health care should have priorities in the allocation of health dollars?

These kinds of questions are raised daily, but as a rule decisions are made by the health-care facility, the doctors and the courts; usually the family's wishes along with the patient's requests have been ignored.

These questions are moral, social and spiritual.

- Do we as human beings have the right to choose to

die with dignity, surrounded by loved ones, rather than live ignominiously through power and the latest masterpiece of technology?

A Young Patient

As hard as it is to make these decisions in behalf of the aged, it is even more difficult in the case of a young person. In Southern California, Christina, a seventeen-year-old high school senior, was in a car accident. She suffered severe head trauma, broken clavicle, broken jaw, shattered hips, ripped bladder, a torn ovary and multiple lacerations, and she was in a deep coma.

Her parents were told she might wake up today, tomorrow, next week or never. Christina's family were fighters. They held a group meeting with all their friends and family and told them there was one rule: No one could enter ICU without a smile on their face and in their voice. Even though Christina was unconscious, the family *knew* there must be no negativism in that hospital room. They kept a three-week vigil on a twenty-four-hour-a-day basis while praying for Christina's complete recovery. During this period the girl also suffered a stroke.

While she was unconscious they chatted with her about the good things in life, as though she could hear. On the thirteenth day she opened her eyes but showed no sign of recognition. A week later she spoke the word, "Mom." What John Sherrill felt to be his mother's ability to hear — though not respond — was also true for Christina. A nurse stated that Christina recovered because the family was positive.

Emerging from a coma is rarely a sudden awakening. It has been likened to the opening of small windows, one at a time with, perhaps, a long interval between openings. Sensory stimulation became the key for Christina as her family talked to her about her schoolmates, the weather — anything to keep the atmosphere positive.

Labor of Love

When her body began to pull into a permanent fetal position, the nurses tied her head up and both of her arms were tied to the bed rails. She also had casts on both legs because her feet began to turn inward. The casts, however, were cut in half to allow her family to take them apart and exercise her legs three to five times a day. Her brother, John, was especially attentive. He spent hours massaging her legs, back and buttocks in a loving, caring way and her vital signs improved each time he worked with her. These loving ministrations prevented permanent paralysis.

It was difficult for Christina's family and friends to keep the required "happy" attitude. They got tired, lost sleep, and did not eat properly — but they never let Christina hear them moan or complain.

It is tough to care for seriously disabled loved ones. It *is* a labor of love and one that in this case proved successful because Christina made a complete recovery. She developed strength in her muscles and improved just as a baby develops by being cuddled and loved.

A Cancer Patient

However, we never know for certain if we can — or how we will — handle situations until we are faced with them. In another part of the country a story made headlines because of the tragedy involved. The story is about a man whose father was terminally ill with cancer. He had been hospitalized for six weeks when the son entered his hospital room with a gun, put it to the nurse's head and ordered her to unplug the machine. The son had previously begged them to do so and they had refused. Ten minutes after the life support was removed the father died.

Members of the family said their father had always told them he did not ever want to be hooked up to machines. However, being in a coma, he was unable to voice his wishes.

As soon as the father was dead, the son gave the gun to the nurse and apologized for what he had done. The police were called and the man was arrested for murder. Even though the doctors said the father had less than a 5 percent chance for recovery, they would not follow the family's request. What a tragedy! Should any situation get to that stage?

As Christians we want to be in the will of God. But is it God's will for a person to be kept alive by mechanical means long after the body—which God created—is "dead"?

Judie Brown, president of the American Life League, was quoted in *USA Today*:

> First it should be said there is never dignity in death itself because death does not make any sense except as part of a larger picture of what human life is all about. When a dying person is cared for lovingly, there is dignity in those that make sure that his or her rights are respected, that basic needs are never denied, not even for a moment.
>
> And what are the basic necessities—the rights—of a person facing death? Obviously food and water, a clean bed, basic hygiene, and, most important, love. None of these alone can cure a disease.
>
> That's just the point. They are not medicine or "treatment." They are simply the basic things everyone is entitled to as a human being.[11]

Entitled to, yes, but then the questions might arise:
- What about a patient's refusal of life support and/or the "basics"?
- Should that request *always* be honored?

A Recovery

A woman begged her husband to let her die with dignity. She did not want to be hooked up to life-support tubes and wires. When life support eventually became necessary, her husband anguished over the situation. He finally asked the court for permission to disconnect the life-support equipment. Thankfully, the court refused, because in less than a week, his wife opened her eyes and has been slowly recovering ever since.

Only God knows what is in store for the human race. The questions raised about life support differ, and so do the answers. Each person must search his heart, his faith and his conscience to direct him in life-and-death decisions.

4 | The Family's Role

> *I have loved you even as the father has loved me. Live within my love . . . I demand that you love each other as much as I love you* (John 15:9,12, TLB).

GOD INSTRUCTS US to honor our mothers and fathers, and points out that there should be harmony in marriages.

If a family has love, honor, obedience, harmony and a personal relationship with the Lord, they will be capable of handling tough decisions when and if the need for them arises. The family can pray for and receive comfort in their decision when it is in harmony with God's plan for their lives.

The prevalence of the fractured family in our society could be a major contributing factor to the large number of elderly people being institutionalized today. The number of two-parent families has decreased and a large percentage of women have joined the work force. Consequently, there is seldom anyone left at home to care for the elderly or infirmed.

The Effect on the Family

In family situations where someone is available, caring for a bedridden or even partially paralyzed person is always accompanied by difficulties. I don't expect praise for the years I took care of my mother, but it *was* a twenty-four-hour-a-day job, and not every marriage can survive that strain. Due to the constancy of my nursing job and the difficulty in finding "sitters," my understanding husband did not have a full-time wife. The fact that our children were grown helped, but that also meant that we were older, which presented us with an additional problem. My strength was drained more quickly, and that made the task more difficult for us both.

For a while one deaconess from our church visited Mom on a regular basis. Mother enjoyed chatting with someone new and I'm sure Bea has earned a front seat in heaven for her devotion to her work. But then the visits stopped. About a year later another woman came up to me in church and said, "You know, Dorothea, your mother has been on my deacon's calling list this year but I didn't bother to visit because I knew she had you."

I said nothing, but in retrospect I believe I should have. Perhaps she needed to be reminded that a new face was always a pleasant change for Mom and a visit by this lady would have meant a few free minutes for me which would have been a lifesaver. This may be an area in our churches that needs to be examined.

The "caring" task was difficult but I'm certain if we could relive our decision, Don and I would still make a home for Mom, and when the time came for the final verdict on life support our choice would remain the same.

However, if and when the time comes that I am unable to live alone, I pray that care facilities will be improved because I do not want to be a burden for our children and their families.

Even so, I'm sure that our children are better people for having watched us care for Mom. Their contribution to making life as pleasant as possible for their grandmother was an experience in personal growth for them.

Families need to be surrounded and filled with love— the *agape* kind of love that means loving the incontinent and/or difficult patient, not just the darling, cuddly baby. That love is part of having a close walk with the Lord.

A Caring Ex-wife

An example is found in this family's story: Early in 1983, John, a troubled thirty-eight-year-old man, drove his car at an excessive speed and hit another car. The impact was so severe that John's car catapulted, spun and rolled over three times. Strapped in by his seat belt, he rode it out. The rescue squad cut him out of the car and rushed him to the nearest trauma center. The impact from the bouncing and rolling car had blown his head open; his nose was in four sections, his entire body a mass of injuries.

John had been divorced from his wife Nancy for eight years, but she felt the Lord wanted her at the hospital with his parents. They agonized while praying for his life.

Although raised in the church, John had been a rebellious young man and his parents worried for fear he had not accepted the Lord as his personal Savior.

The evening before the accident John had visited Nancy and their children. His six-foot-three frame had towered over Nancy as he entered the home and grabbed her in a bear hug, a movement so out of character that she was startled. For the eight years of their separation there had been no physical contact whatever.

"What is this—some new kind of drug you're taking?" Nancy asked John. She explained to me that she had been kidding, but his performance had seemed weird after all those years.

He explained that he needed to talk to her alone. They walked around the block for privacy while he poured out his heart, confessed his sins and asked what he should do.

"I told him," she continued, "'you are right in confessing these things, but if you give your heart to the Lord, He will be with you. God will forgive you . . . if you are sincere. God will also stand beside you to face these actions.'"

Back at the house while sitting at the dining room table he hung his head, extended his hands palms up and again asked, "What shall I do?"

"Just surrender your life to the Lord," she replied as she took his hands and held them. Then she prayed, "Lord, hear the cry of John's heart. Come into him now and re-store him to You." She didn't ask him to repeat the prayer after her because she feared he might rebel after so many years of disobedience.

He said nothing, just remained with his head down. "It was the *first* time we'd prayed together," she said, with a sob in her voice "the first time since we prayed at the altar on the day of our wedding fourteen years before."

Nancy was quiet a moment, and then she told of put-ting her hands on John's head and how she again asked the Lord to be with him (the head that twenty-four hours later would be severely injured).

John's Finest Ministry

The magnificent part of her story is that the next day when she sat in the hospital with John's mother she was able to share this story and reassure the mother that John *had* given his heart to the Lord. John's mother knew how close Nancy walked with the Lord and was blessed by her reassurance.

The doctors gave the family no encouragement. The prognosis was grim. As they waited, they wondered if they would be forced into making a decision about life support. Could they "pull the plug" if the doctors were certain there was no hope?

To the surprise of the hospital staff, John lived. He was comatose, but alive. Later, when weaned off the respirator, he was able to breathe on his own. He is still being fed through a gastrostomy tube into his stomach. Today he weighs only 85 pounds but his weight is maintained with a 4000-calorie diet. The hole for his tracheotomy never closed and the nurses are able to suction the fluid and mucous from his lungs through that opening. Nancy reports he receives magnificent care at a VA Hospital and despite the fact that he has little flesh on his bones he has never had a sign of a bedsore.

When I asked Nancy if she would ever get to the point of consenting to the withdrawal of his nutrients, she replied, "Personally, I would say never! When God decides to take him that will be fine, but no way would I ever order the feeding to stop. However, now we are praying that God will take him home. His brain damage is so severe that he will never become a whole person. But to 'pull the plug'? No, not unless God gave me that order!

"I stood alone in my belief that he would be healed, and he has stayed alive longer than they thought possible. He is no longer comatose. He turns his head when you speak but his eyes do not see. We don't know how much he understands. The head nurse stated that he has the mentality of a three-month old.

"A doctor said to me after John was transferred to the VA Hospital, 'You know there is no hope, don't you?' "

Nancy replied, "No, I don't! He is breathing, so there is hope! As long as there is breath in his lungs, God has a purpose for his living. John's finest ministry has been performed from that bed. There have been reconciliations that no one will ever know about.

"I can't count the number of miracles that have resulted from John's accident. Lives have been touched, and problems within families have been healed. He has been the source of wonders for which he will be rewarded.

"I was called by the family of an accident victim who had heard about John," she continued, "and was asked to pray for their son. I went to the hospital, talked with the family, answered questions and then went into the young man's room to pray. Even though the prognosis gave no hope, he eventually came out of his coma. Today he is well."

I asked Nancy, "Do you feel life-support systems should stay on indefinitely, even when physicians say there is no hope, when it means pushing nutrients into a body that is literally dead? When the patient is brain dead, too?"

Nancy answered, "I don't fault a person who decides

when a loved one is brain dead to stop the heroic measures, but John isn't brain dead. He has suffered severe brain damage. He's like a baby lying in bed with no concern for his needs. Once when he had a look of fear on his face, I stroked his forehead, sang and read to him from the Bible and watched his facial muscles relax."

This experience paralleled the reaction Mrs. Sherrill showed when her son read psalms to her. We have no way of knowing what the human brain can absorb when asleep, unconscious, comatose or—as in John's case—severely damaged.

A Distressing End

The idea of making life-and-death rulings baffles any family, especially one which is not involved in the healing and helping professions.

In another life-or-death situation, a volunteer who worked with refugee programs befriended an Indonesian extended family. One day the grandmother collapsed on the street and was rushed to the hospital, but her family could not be located. She was hooked up to life-support systems but further treatment was delayed. When her family discovered she was hospitalized they asked their volunteer friend to go to the hospital with them. The grandmother had suffered a massive stroke and was comatose.

The family did not understand what had happened. They thought their grandmother indestructible. After weeks of indecision, and with no pattern on the brain scan, the family decided to accept the doctor's opinion that she was already dead and the respirator should be removed.

The woman who had helped them told me of the experience when the respirator was removed. "Her body began to convulse; she sounded as though she was gasping for breath. The family screamed to turn the respirator back on, but it would have been to no avail. They still do not understand what happened, nor do I."

As she told the story she shuddered, took a deep breath, then continued, "I relive their shock and mine every time

I tell this story. It was horrible! I had no idea that could happen. We presumed she would just lie there as she had for those many weeks and quietly die."

Dignity for the Patient

What is the answer?

Some people would put the decision on a par with how we treat animals — those influenced by humanistic arguments, for instance. Some answers you are likely to hear would be similar to what appeared in the *Wall Street Journal* in an article by Alan L. Otten. He reflected:

> When I was a boy, my family had a beloved bulldog. Eventually he became very old — blind, incontinent, wheezing heavily, barely able to eat or walk. We took him to the vet and as the euphemism then had it, the vet "put Jerry to sleep."
>
> Every few days now I go to visit my 90-year-old mother in a nearby nursing home, more to salve my own conscience probably than to do her any meaningful service. For her, in fact, there is little I can do. She lies on her side in bed, legs drawn rigidly into a fetal position, blinks at me uncomprehendingly as I prattle on about family doings, and she rarely utters a sound except a shriek of pain when the attendants turn her from one side to the other in their constant battle to heal her horrible bed sores. She must be hand-fed, and her incontinency requires a urethral catheter.
>
> Why do we treat our aged and beloved animals better than we treat our aged and loved human beings? Shouldn't a humane, caring society — as ours is supposed to be — begin to consider ways to put my long-suffering mother and the steadily growing number of miserable others like her, peacefully to sleep?[1]

On March 17, 1986, Nancy Dickey, chairwoman of the American Medical Association's Council on Ethical and Judicial Affairs, released this statement:

> For humane reasons, with informed consent, a physician may do what is medically necessary to alleviate severe pain, or cease or omit treatment to permit a terminally ill patient whose death is imminent to die. However, he should not intentionally cause death . . .

Even if death is not imminent but a patient's coma is beyond doubt irreversible and there are adequate safeguards to confirm the accuracy of the diagnosis and with the concurrence of those who have responsibility for the care of the patient, it is not unethical to discontinue all means of life-prolonging medical treatment.

Life-prolonging medical treatment includes medication and artificially or technologically supplied respirators, nutrition or hydration. In treating a terminally ill or irreversibly comatose patient, the physician should determine whether the benefits of the treatment outweigh its burdens. At all times, the dignity of the patient should be maintained.[2]

But who sets the standards for "dignity"? What doctor or family member has enough wisdom for the task?

Jesus promised: "I will never leave thee, nor forsake thee" (Hebrews 13:5b, KJV), reminding us again that God is always available. However, to be certain the right decision is reached in these life-and-death situations, it is best to have a doctor, a lawyer, a pastor and an uninvolved person present with the family. Each individual should explain his recommendation. Preferably the decision will be unanimous, but the family, with God's guidance, should make the final determination.

"Pro-life" and "Pro-freedom of choice" examined

| 5 | Bioethical Issues |

5 Bioethical Issues

> *Oh, why should light and life be given to those in misery and bitterness, who long for death, and it won't come; who search for death as others search for food or money? What blessed relief when at last they die!*
> (Job 3:20-22, TLB)

IN 1978 A three-year-old boy was hit by a car. Critically injured, he was rushed to a hospital where, because he was unable to breathe, he was put on a respirator. He had suffered severe brain damage and the doctors recommended that he would not be helped by continuing the life-support system. The grieving family accepted the fact and were willing to leave the child in God's hands. However, the Los Angeles Times reported: "In order to avoid a possible lawsuit, the hospital's attorney recommended that the hospital obtain a court order" before the removal of any equipment.

In a closed court hearing *three months later,* the judge called in as many doctors as possible to testify about the medical situation. This was a devastating experience for an already suffering family. The family had no funds, the father had lost his job because of the situation, and guardianship of the child had been taken from them to prevent them from "pulling the plug" before the court reached a decision.

It was finally decided that the respirator could be removed; the child was allowed to die.

Ethics Committees

This painful experience proved to Sister Corrine Bayley that courts should not be involved in these decisions and that hospitals needed a forum for decision making.[1] Recognized as an expert in the field of bioethics, Bayley asks for a new approach to these heart-wrenching decisions.

About 30 percent of the nation's hospitals now have ethics committees which are equipped to help families who face these life-or-death situations. This is an improvement over the 1978 position, but there are still problems. The physician cannot abdicate his role, yet he needs to know when it is time to stop. A patient can be treated until he is a sixty-pound skeleton, and the physician can justify the action medically. But what about morally? There has to be a point at which medical treatment is proven not only unnecessary but cruel.

It has been said that death is the *only* certainty in life: The sole indisputable fact of life is that we all must die. Yet death is not the enemy . . . it is the inhuman way in which many die that makes death tragic.

Medical science and technology have increased a person's life expectancy dramatically, and no one would suggest changing that. The ethic behind the use of this technology, though, has been the belief that everything possible must be done to prevent death. Actually these techniques often do not prevent death; they only prolong the dying process.

In the third chapter of this book you read true stories of families who profess Christianity; yet their beliefs on life support differ. The subject does not have clear black and white values. There are too many gray areas. The one thing that is certain is that *to die with dignity, surrounded by family and friends rather than tubes, machines and doctors, is the wish of almost everyone.*

In making life-or-death decisions, there are two basic Christian schools of thought: (1) strict pro-life; and (2) consideration on the basis of the quality of the life.

PRO-LIFE

In *Beneficent Euthanasia,* Bertram and Elsie Bandham ask, What is so beneficent about death or alleviation of suffering? They suggest that one has to consider the possibility of a new medical discovery or drug that will cure or put a disease in remission—a discovery that might be found the day after a plug is pulled.

"A Process—Not a Right"

In their opinion, "Death is the termination of the process of life; it is necessary and inevitable, not a freedom and so not a right." They continue by stating that death is not a virtue under almost all circumstances, except possibly in cases of heroism where someone else benefits. To them death is something no one would desire. They further point out that with death we cease to have any connection with the world, that death means "the annihilation of a person. To be dead is not to be." (Fortunately, for the Christian the future is much more hopeful than this.)

They explain that there is no "good death." Even when in extreme pain, they believe a person would prefer to be rid of the disease rather than to die. "Even those who welcome death seldom do so in the belief that death is another phase of a better life rather than the end of life."[2]

Questioning Euthanasia

In *To Live and Die: When, Why, and How,* Arthur J. Dyck asks, What ethic guides those who support euthanasia? "The ethic designated as the old ethic, rooted in Judaism and Christianity, is treated as an impediment to medicine's effort to improve quality of life."

The argument for compassion, Dyck points out, usually attacks the "inhumanity of keeping dying people alive when they are in great pain" or unable to function as usual. But he asks, What is the result of the "medical practice of promoting or even encouraging direct acts on the part of physicians to shorten the lives of their patients?"

The author continues, "There is nothing in the Jewish or Christian tradition that provides an exact blueprint as to what is the most compassionate thing to do for someone who is dying."

By advocating the termination of suffering, or allowing a person to commit suicide while a doctor looks on, will this not make the physician a partner to that suicide? Will the next step be asking or allowing physicians to use chemicals or instruments to bring about death?

Dyck asks another pointed question: If one means of shortening life is acceptable, then do we accept any and all means? This focuses on the consequences rather than the aim.

The book quotes from Joseph Fletcher's writings and questions Fletcher's belief in the "freedom of a patient to choose how and when he or she will die."

Dyck states that the ethic that defends suicide is from both the Stoics and the Epicureans who "considered the choice of one's own death as the ultimate expression of freedom . . . dignity . . . and personhood." If a Stoic were threatened by death, he would choose to die rather than to fear it.

Dyck continues by referring to the Ten Commandments which include: "Thou shalt not kill." He points out the importance of this commandment to both the Jewish and Christian personage. He further states that it is part of "a total effort to prevent the destruction of the human community," and that under it any act of taking a life would be wrong.

Dyck does, however, believe in *benemortasia*, an invented term that says death does not need to be painless or induced in order to be good. What makes a good or happy death is disputable.

Distinctions

This ethic recognizes the freedom of a patient to refuse

medical intervention in his dying process, but does not accept suicide or assisted suicide as a valid act. Dyck feels there is a profound distinction between acts that permit death and acts that cause death.

He further summarizes by stating that euthanasia is morally wrong and that no conscientious physician could participate in such an act. He believes that both Jewish and Christian heritages declare that life and selfhood are not ours to dispose of as we see fit.[3]

H. Richard Neibuhr questions whether we even *can* dispose of ourselves:

> I live but do not have the power to live. And further, I may die at any moment but am powerless to die. It was not my power, nor in my parents' power, to elect my *self* into existence. Though they willed a child, or consented to it, they did not will *me*.
>
> I can destroy the life of my body. Can I destroy myself? This remains the haunting question of the literature of suicide and of all the lonely debates of men to whom existence becomes a burden. Whether they shall wake up again, either here in this life or there in some other mode of being, is beyond their control. We can choose many alternatives, but the power to choose self-existence or self-extinction is not ours. Men can practice birth-control, not self-creation; they can commit biocide; whether they can commit suicide, self-destruction, remains a question.[4]

Destructive practices of "euthanasia" as recorded in this century's history have given rise to genuine fear. In *Death by Decision*, Jerry B. Wilson discusses Nazi Germany's sense of freedom to "kill at will."

He says that what happened in Germany in the 1930s and early 1940s undoubtedly influenced Dietrich Bonhoeffer. He took a strong stand in which he claimed there were only two arguments for euthanasia, "consideration for the sick and consideration for the healthy," and neither were convincing. "Arguments for euthanasia out of regard for the incurably sick must predispose their assent or wish to die . . . and it can hardly be said that the patient is being considered when this desire is not expressed or when there is an unmistakable demand to remain alive."

Bonhoeffer claims that "in the sight of God there is no life that is not worth living."[5]

PRO-FREEDOM OF CHOICE

On the other hand, Marvin Kohl contends in *Beneficent Euthanasia*: "The question of whether or not an act of passive euthanasia is sinful or immoral" isn't apt to occur unless one believes that in all instances to continue living is an "absolute or intrinsic good."

To state emphatically that *all* human life is intrinsically good is to say that every person's life is good. This says that even the life of a child born with major defects who survived and was deaf, blind and retarded, and had multiple other irregularities . . . that his life is intrinsically good. It says that *every* life, no matter what physical, mental or psychological problem is involved, is intrinsically good. "The flaw in that position lies not in its intention but in its results," Kohl contends. It accepts pointless suffering.

Again, I do not necessarily embrace this author's position, but I am presenting it to help you understand the differing viewpoints you will encounter.

Kohl further claims that "in certain circumstances we have an actual moral obligation to induce death." We have to choose and act in ways we believe to be in the best interest of the individual. No person should suffer simply because he or she is unable to give consent.

He goes on to tell of a time when he was approached by a clergyman who heard him speak on euthanasia. The clergyman was upset and explained that he refused to believe that God had created a world where it was necessary to ever kill an innocent human being. This objection puzzled Kohl because "it turns upon the failure to face reality — the refusal to accept the fact that death may be a kindness."[6]

Even Gandhi, the father of twentieth-century pacifism and a man who abhorred violence and almost all forms of killing, wrote: "I see there is an instinctive horror of kill-

ing living beings under any circumstances whatever . . .
[But] should my child be attacked with rabies and there
was no helpful remedy to relieve his agony, I should consider it my duty to take his life . . . [For] one of the
remedies and the final one to relieve the agony of a tortured
child is to take his life."[7]

The same feeling can hold true toward others in an
individual's family. In *The Summer of the Great
Grandmother*, Madeline L'Engle tells of the mixed emotions she felt as she watched her mother deteriorate:

> I love my mother, not as a prisoner of atherosclerosis,
> but as a person; and I must love her enough to accept her
> as she is, now, for as long as this dwindling may take; and
> I must love her enough, when the time comes to let her
> go into a new birth, a new life of which I can know noth-
> ing, and which I cannot prove; a new life which may not
> be; but of which I have had enough intimations so that I
> cannot discount its possibility, no matter how difficult
> such a possibility is for the intellect.[8]

Alzheimer's Disease

Facing death or dying is not easy, and its degree of difficulty can depend largely on one's relationship with God.
During the writing of this book, Robert Young portrayed
Roswell Gilbert in the television play, "Mercy or Murder."
As I watched him shoot his wife, go through the horror of
the trial and be found guilty of murder, I wept for both Roswell Gilbert and his wife.

To kill her was wrong—few would argue that point. The
Bible states: "Thou shalt not kill," and Gilbert did . . .
but he was in the proverbial position of being between a
rock and a hard place. I feel certain that I could not have
done what he did; but until a person has faced the same
situation, he does not know what he might do.

Mrs. Roswell's life was miserable . . . and his was,
too. No gracious, loving God invented Alzheimer's disease.
Situations such as this prove that Satan is alive and well in
our world today.

I read of another woman who suffered with Alzheimer's

disease. She became so depressed that she begged her husband, "Throw me away, I'm no good." Her husband had
watched his wife of forty years change from a lively,
pleasant companion into a frightened stranger, a child in
the body of a woman. The frustration of being unable to
stop the progression of the disease is devastating and the
patient can live to experience many years of deterioration.

There are over a million cases of Alzheimer's disease
today and the prognosis is scary. As the family of another
Alzheimer patient said, "Cancer is a tangible pain, but with
this disease there is only a feeling of helplessness." Although not really a terminal illness, it is one that can
bankrupt and/or destroy a family by the devastation of its
unpredictability.

So the same questions surface over and over again. Is
it God's will to allow bodies to be hooked up to machines
and equipment to save lives or perhaps to only prolong the
dying process? Is it God's will for us to fight to stay alive or
to keep someone else alive no matter what?

6 | Meeting the Need

> *For everything there is a season, and a time for every matter under heaven: a time to be born, and a time to die* (Ecclesiastes 3:1,2a, RSV).

THE GRANDMOTHER of my friend Ann was in her nineties when she suffered a heart attack. At the hospital the doctors explained that by-pass surgery was the only way to extend her life. There are eleven children in the family and all — except Ann's father — agreed with the grandmother's wish to be sent home to die. Ann's father did not want to lose his mother. She was the matriarchal figure who had ruled their family with a combination of love and strength.

However, Ann's father was overruled and had no choice but to agree with the ten others. Grandmother returned home to enjoy her large family for several months before a massive heart attack took her home to the Lord.

"Death Is Momentous"

Life holds no guarantees, yet death is often difficult to face and understand. As Christians we have to deal with the theological precepts that surround death.

In his book, *Life, Death and Destiny,* Roger Lincoln Shinn discusses facts about the Bible's attitude toward life and death. He says, "It does not recommend a casual, philosophic attitude toward death. For death is momentous." He explains that we don't decide to be born or to die but we're so afraid of death that when we express sympathy to the bereaved we try to help them forget death rather than face it with courage.[1]

God promises another life — one where we will know His plans.

> Then the eyes of the blind shall be opened, and the ears of the deaf unstopped; then shall the lame man leap like a deer, and the tongue of the dumb sing for joy (Isaiah 35:5,6a, RSV).

> He will swallow up death for ever, and the Lord GOD will wipe away tears from all faces, and the reproach of his people he will take away from all the earth for the LORD has spoken (Isaiah 25:8, RSV).

> So that, just as sin reigned in death, so also grace might reign through righteousness to bring eternal life through Jesus Christ our Lord (Romans 5:21, NIV).

In *Concerning Them That Are Asleep,* Daniel Hoffman Martin shares a reassuring thought:

> The question Job asked in his despair finds an echo in many a human heart: "If a man die, shall he live again?" Who has stood by an open grave where the form of a loved one was lowered into the gloomy depths and not asked the same question? But death is not an enemy. Death is the decree of our loving Father, who takes this method of giving us an exchange of worlds.
> Job's question, the question of every grief-stricken heart, is met by the word of Jesus: "Because I live, ye shall live also."
> The grave is but a hyphen between two worlds.[2]

Concern for Human Need

Joseph Fletcher explains in *Beneficent Euthanasia* that the basis of pastoral care and ministry is a loving concern for human needs. There should be no distinction between pastoral theology and Christian ethics. "Christian ethics is agapistic," he writes, which means centered in love, not law. He believes that pastoral theology and moral theology encompass each other.

Fletcher asks: "Which come first, rights or needs?" His ethical stance is that "needs have precedence over rights." But "to be candid and careful about the subject," he goes on to explain that he is "not primarily concerned about any supposed right to live or supposed right to die; I am primarily concerned with human *need* — both of life and of death."[3]

In *Whatever Happened to the Human Race?* Francis Schaeffer and C. Everett Koop, M.D., discuss the "inhuman era" in which we live: "Cultures can be judged in many ways, but eventually every nation in every age must be judged by this test: *How did it treat people?*"[4]

They explain that, although the Hippocratic oath is from the Greeks, the real concept of sanctity of life is from Judeo-Christian teachings.

> Biblical doctrine was preached not as *a* truth but as *the* truth. That is, it provided the basic moral and social values by which things are judged.
>
> Why has our society changed? The answer is clear: The consensus of our society no longer rests on a Judeo-Christian base, but rather on a humanistic one. Humanism makes man "the measure of all things." It puts man rather than God at the center of things.[5]
>
> The question is not the worth of the imperfect infant, the retarded child, the defective adult, and the aging individual with physical and mental signs of the aging process. The question is this: Are we worthy enough to extend ourselves to meet their needs?[6]

When we must make life-and-death decisions we can be helped by talking to others who have walked the same path. In my own case, I searched the Scriptures when Mom begged me not to call the paramedics; I couldn't just sit in a chair and watch her die. So I called them. But oh, how I prayed . . . and that was my salvation. God promises to give us no more than we can handle, and He *always* keeps His promises. I often felt like running away, but prayer and a consistent daily quiet time gave me the strength to continue. I was emotionally drained — but able to cope.

Responses of Religious Men

Pondering why these things happen and where to find answers led me to ask several pastors, a theologian and a priest some pertinent questions. One of the questions was:

When you are asked by a family about the use of life support, what do you tell them?

Here are their answers:

PASTOR A (from southern California):
I stress three things. First, every person should make out a living will, putting into writing what his wishes are. Typical formats for such wills are available from a variety of sources. [See appendix A.]

Second, the spiritual condition of the person in question should be evaluated. For one who is born again, Psalm 116:15 applies: "Precious in the sight of the LORD is the death of his saints" (KJV). On the other hand, if we believe that the one who dies without Christ is eternally lost, any further opportunity to respond to the gospel cannot be treated lightly.

Finally, what commitments have been made already between family members? Obviously, great care should be taken in making promises. But once made, integrity becomes an issue.

THEOLOGIAN (from Colorado):
It depends on the circumstances. Are you dealing with someone who is comatose, unable to enter the discussion, and are you dealing with a situation in which the patient has *not* expressed his will or desire? If the patient has (as one of my friends did) expressed his desire before the development of a situation like that, then I think that would be a very important factor. Let's assume the doctor said there is absolutely no hope and feels it may drag on for a long time, and the individual has said he would prefer not to have his life artificially prolonged . . . then I would turn off the equipment.

PASTOR B (from eastern California):
If I am asked about the use of life-support systems, my response is constructed around the biblical concept of hope. Medically, is there hope for the patient? If the life-support systems will buy time for a more promising

medical intervention, then I'd encourage the use of those systems. If they only postpone the inevitable without hope of any appreciable amelioration of the problem, then I would not advocate their use.

On the other hand, the concept of hope is family-focused as well. While there may be little or no hope for the patient, if the family can be encouraged and time bought for their needed adjustments to the coming reality, then I would advocate the use of such systems.

As you can see, the crucial word in my paradigm is "hope." How can we as mere humans with our categorical limitations know whether there might be a miraculous intervention by God if we only hold on, pray and have faith? My answer is that we cannot know these things, and must, therefore, proceed on our best knowledge and understanding at the time. We, as Christians, have the mind of Christ and sometimes we simply must make a decision by faith, and trust that it is correct.

PASTOR C (from southern California):

If, in the considered judgment of the doctor and others on the medical staff, heroic and costly steps could not lead to any chance for meaningful existence, I would give support to their decision to decline their use, or withdraw them. I would need to be sensitive to how heavy their feelings of guilt might be afterward, but I feel this can be dealt with best in terms of whether their loved one would want to be alive "but not live."

Sometimes the pain is eased if an accident has produced the critical condition and the person's organs can save someone else's life. I have been with families at such times.

In terms of one's Christian convictions, I would share my own personal belief that Jesus, who gives power to heal and who wants us to be well, also affirms the reality of our mortality. But that isn't "all there is." The opportunity to express one's belief in a life in Christ free of bodily inhibitions is also possible.

PASTOR D (from the Midwest):

It is, of course, their decision and theirs alone, but the input of medical personnel and clergy can be most helpful.

A question for them to consider, from a philosophical

and theological perspective, is, What constitutes full human life? It might be of help to point out that maintaining biological functions may be something less than full human life in which the person is a responding individual, capable of interaction.

PRIEST (from the Midwest):
Life support covers a wide range of treatment and technology, even though all of it aims to prolong life. The Catholic tradition, recently affirmed by the Vatican Declaration on Euthanasia, would assess the proposal to use life-support measures within the distinction between proportionate and disproportionate means of treatment. This distinction has been commonly recognized as ordinary or extraordinary. But these are misleading terms. They too easily obscure where and on whom we ought to focus attention in order to make clinical judgments. Proportionality seems to express this distinction more clearly because it focuses on the relationship between the effects of the treatment and the benefit the patient will experience. Understanding this distinction helps us appreciate the difference between treatment which truly prolongs life and that which merely prolongs dying.
In light of this distinction then, I would want the family to determine first the patient's wishes. Hopefully he or she would have expressed these wishes in a formal document or explicitly through conversation. If his wishes are unknown, the family has to judge in the best interest of the patient. The judgment should include the nature of the life-support measure with risks and benefits it may bring, the degree of incapacity it may cause, the projected length and kind of life the patient would experience as a result, and the impact of that life on family and society.

The answers of these various religious professionals are varied, yet the same thread of the need for God to be in charge is woven through all of the replies.

Illumination From the Holy Spirit

The ethical issues in health care are as varied as the terminal illnesses that commit us to the doorway of death. The Christian turns to the Bible for answers. Paul wrote that to die is gain.

In *Making Ethical Decisions*, Howard Clark Kee discusses the dilemmas involved. He explains that making choices according to "Christian" convictions is not simple. Each decision usually leads to another that is perhaps even more difficult, and the Protestant Christian has no commonly accepted rules for making ethical decisions.

The old way of asking oneself, "What would Jesus do?" does not often help. According to Kee, Jesus' situations differed in specific issues because of cultural differences and there is no direct or automatic way of transferring His teachings to fit every present-day situation.[7]

Even in our advanced, scientific, computerized world there is no button we can push for a prompt and guaranteed correct answer.

However, Kee maintains that the way in which Jesus provided His followers with moral insights in making decisions is still available to help us wrestle through our problems. He points out that "one of Jesus' major concerns in dealing with his contemporaries was to destroy the prideful complacency that led them to suppose they had a corner on God's favor because they observed the law of Moses."[8]

Kee goes on to say that "we cannot treat the New Testament as though it were a set of correct answers given at the back of a mathematics text to show us whether we are right or wrong." He then reminds the reader that the Holy Spirit is available today to illumine the minds and energize the wills of those who seek to do God's will.[9]

Hippocrates, the father of modern medicine, wrote his principles of medical science four hundred years before the birth of Christ. The Hippocratic oath named for him stresses the importance of relieving suffering and protecting life. He applied logic and reason to medicine, but took the treatment of disease out of the area of religion. However, if one believes in God, religion has to be a part of everything. It was God who created us and who created the world.

Isaiah reminds us that

the Lord who created you, O Israel, says, Don't be afraid, for I have ransomed you; I have called you by name; you are mine. When you go through deep waters and great trouble, I will be with you. When you go through rivers of difficulty, you will not drown! When you walk through the fire of oppression, you will not be burned up—the flames will not consume you (Isaiah 43:1,2, TLB).

What promises! What security for those who know and walk with the Lord. He will guide us; He will be with our loved ones who suffer; and He will show us the way if we but wait on Him. He will give us the answers, though we may have to search for them and learn patience in the process.

However, as He shows us the way, we must realize there are a variety of routes possible—alternatives for the care of the terminally ill, options that need to be considered, examined and prayed about.

7 Alternatives

> *Love bears all things, believes all things, hopes all things, endures all things* (1 Corinthians 13:7, RSV).

A LINE FROM an old song goes, "Love makes the world go round." Love is also the key to making choices when the care of the infirmed is in question.

When faced with making decisions for one who is seriously ill, there are two ways to demonstrate love: (1) to release the person from a suffering or comatose state; and (2) to be firm in a decision to maintain life as long as possible with whatever means are available through medical science and technology. Whichever route is favored, the important thing is to follow the wishes of the patient if at all possible.

Madeline L'Engle says regarding society today, "One of the worst things about our attitude toward old people is the assumption that they ought to be herded together with other old people." She then tells about her grandfather who lived to be 101. He played golf until he was 95, always with younger men — who usually were not able to keep up with him. He complained that people his age could not do things with him.[1]

That is the way most people would like to travel

through the aging process, but few will be that fortunate. When the time does arrive that a loved one is unable to continue living as an independent person, changes must be considered.

The decisions are usually devastating and people often ask, "Where is God?" The Bible assures us that God is not responsible for sickness, suffering and death—they are the result of sin in the world. These things are not tolerated in the New Testament. Jesus healed the sick, as did His disciples after they were indwelt by the Holy Spirit.

Many theologians believe that when Paul and other New Testament writers speak of sharing the suffering of Christ, they are not talking about physical illness but about the persecution they suffered from the Romans and Jews because of their beliefs. "For as we share abundantly in Christ's sufferings, so through Christ we share abundantly in comfort too" (2 Corinthians 1:5, RSV).

Then in Hebrews 2:9,10, we are told:

> But we see Jesus, who for a little while was made lower than the angels, crowned with glory and honor because of the suffering of death, so that by the grace of God he might taste death for every one. For it was fitting that he, for whom and by whom all things exist, in bringing many sons to glory, should make the pioneer of their salvation perfect through suffering (RSV).

We can conclude, then, that physical suffering and death do not necessarily glorify God. He loves us too much to find pleasure in our pain, so it is logical for us to do whatever we can to relieve suffering. When the time comes that a care facility is needed, we need to know about the available alternatives.

Options

Following is a discussion of the major options families have at "decision time." As stated previously, the first consideration must be the patient. What does he or she want, need or require? Situations differ. If possible, it is important for families to discuss these possibilities before the need arises. It is easier to be candid with one another before emotions run rampant—which makes the determination much more difficult.

1. MAJOR or ACUTE-CARE HOSPITAL:

The hospital which treats the person who requires surgery or is seriously ill. An intensive care unit (ICU) is available, and the ratio of registered nurses to aides is much higher than in other facilities.

The patient is treated and cared for here until he (or she) no longer needs major or acute hospital care, or sometimes, until insurance coverage stops. At that time he will need to be moved to another type of facility if he is unable to return to independent living.

2. CONVALESCENT HOSPITAL:

A facility for the less seriously ill than those in the acute-care hospital but for those who still require round-the-clock nursing. The supervised care provided in this facility is often termed "custodial" by insurance companies to prevent them from being responsible for the costs involved. (We found this to be the case with our mother.) The patients are bedridden, or they are able to be up in a wheelchair only, or they may be ambulatory but unable to function without close supervision.

Convalescent hospitals provide a more intensive level of nursing than is possible in home care, but they still may not be a desirable choice. My advice is to check the convalescent hospitals out thoroughly with doctors or friends—anyone who knows anything about the facility— before your family makes a decision.

Recently I spoke with a friend from my working days. Her mother is in the same care facility I had visited and thought so excellent. Her opinion differed from mine. In addition to paying $2200 per month for a two-bed room, she has to visit every day to be certain her mother gets the needed care.

Her mother is physically fine but mentally confused. My friend found her last week sitting in her wheelchair in a totally dark room. It was evening but not yet bedtime.

Unable to turn on a light, she was still dressed and her tray of food sat uneaten. It is sad when aged loved ones are not given the TLC they especially need. My friend said she usually visited on Sunday afternoon, but that day she had been unable to get there until evening. She felt that her mother was neglected because the care facility thought she would not visit that day.

In defense of these facilities, though, one doctor said, "Convalescent hospitals are so understaffed that when families complain about the care their parents are getting, I tell them to go in and help. When one aide has eight to ten patients and three of them have to be fed, she can't keep up with the work. Too many families 'dump' their infirmed in the hospital and forget them. That's another reason these places are depressing to visit. They need the sound of happy voices and of young people."

Pet Therapy

Last week I visited a new facility in this area where the grandmother of one of the young married couples in our church resides. I was awed! The floors shone like diamonds, the smell was fresh and sweet, many nurses and aides bustled around, and they even had Freckles, a large black and white dog, ambling in and out of the patients' rooms. He allowed each person the opportunity to pat him and to chat with him for a few moments.

Research has proven the effectiveness of allowing a care facility to use "pet therapy" for their patients. Freckles made that facility a home away from home and the lady I visited could say only good things about the loving care the nursing staff gave her. Prior to her stay here, she had been in the same facility my dad was in ten years earlier. The care there was still dreadful, she reported.

Skilled Care and Intermediate Care

Two other facilities much like convalescent hospitals and most often part of a health care system are *skilled care* and *intermediate care* facilities. The primary care provided here involves assistance with medication, bathing, and general supervision of personal needs. Although twenty-four-hour professional nursing care is sometimes available, these facilities are not licensed, equipped nor intended for the bedridden or handicapped person.

3. BOARD AND CARE HOME:

Here the residents are more capable than those in convalescent hospitals or intermediate and skilled care facilities, but they are unable to live alone. Their meals are prepared for them, their rooms are cleaned, and their activities receive general supervision. The residents must be ambulatory and capable of taking care of their own medication.

Some private households have been licensed as board-and-care homes, but you must be careful. Many of them are good ones, but some are deplorable. The *Orange County Register* recently ran a week-long exposé of board-and-care homes. The negatives outnumbered the positives by such a high percentage that it frightens me to realize I am nearing the age when those facilities may become a part of my life.

4. RETIREMENT HOME or RESIDENTIAL CARE:

This level is for those who are capable of caring for themselves and are competent enough to live independently but who want the security that is not available when living alone. Food and housekeeping services are supplied. The individual must be able to function without the aid of a walker or wheelchair and be mentally alert enough to go out for meals when desired or to shop and travel, and they may still have their car. This type of facility provides the residents with a nominally supervised independence.

If the patient is healthy but fearful or in need of supportive company, the retirement home should be the first consideration. They are expensive but if money is not a problem, most people who enter these facilities are happy, well-fed and cared for.

In researching types of facilities available I discovered that today some retirement and board-and-care homes have incorporated both intermediate and convalescent hospital areas for their guests. With this arrangement the patient moves to whatever area of care is required but within the same facility. This saves the family the grief of relocating the patient. Many of these are church affiliated and the care is excellent. Here again, it is wise to search them out before the need arises because the good ones have waiting lists.

Checking Them Out

If the possibility of this or any other care-facility need looms in the not-too-far-future, start right now to check those that are available. Visit them unannounced. What is the neighborhood like? Is a good church nearby? Notice how the home smells, and look over the condition of the residents, their rooms, the dining room and the kitchen. Is there an activity room or activity director? Ask if you may pay for and eat a meal with the residents. If not, at least visit at mealtime to check the menu and see how it is being served. That is an excellent way to reach a decision.

Some years back a widow friend of mine signed up and entered a very nice care-facility home while she was still able to drive and travel. The adjustment was made and new friends were acquired before she lost her sight and became dependent on others. It has been much easier for her than for some others I know. It pays to look and plan ahead.

5. HOME CARE:

A way to avoid all of the above except acute hospital care. Home care is for the family who decides to care for a loved one themselves, in their home. This care would be the least expensive and is usually the most desirable choice for the patient. However, it involves a great deal of love and dedication on the part of the caretakers, who usually are the patient's family. The considerations are many:

a. Is the patient ambulatory?

b. Is the caretaker strong enough to handle any lifting that is or may become necessary?

c. Does the caretaker have the patience necessary to handle the pressures that may be involved?

d. Can the patient get in and out of a tub or shower?

e. If the patient needs a walker or wheelchair, are ramps available? And be sure to check the width of the bathroom and bedroom doors!

f. Can the patient feed himself? To feed three meals a day is time consuming.

g. What about personal hygiene? Cleaning a baby's soft firm bottom is almost pleasant, but an elderly wrinkled bottom can be difficult.

h. Do you have an alternate caretaker, someone who can be on call?

i. Are you prepared to face the reality that someday you may reach a point where you can no longer handle the care? Don't go on a guilt trip when and if that happens!

A Sense of Humor

If the decision has been reached to try home care, then consider handrails in the hallways, a buzzer in the patient's room to call for help, and NO scatter rugs any place. One of the main requirements I learned from our experience was the necessity of maintaining a sense of humor through it all. I remember the night Mom's buzzer blasted in the middle of the night. Our bedroom was upstairs and I flew out of bed, tore down the stairs, hearing the buzzer blare all the way. I turned on Mom's light and asked, "What's the matter?"

She yawned and replied, "Why are you here? I didn't call."

My reaction was not as Christian as it should have been. "Then why on earth did you push the buzzer like a panic button?"

She looked down and realized she had the buzzer in her hand, and had no answer.

"OK," I replied, "let's both try to get back to sleep." I fumed in silence as I trudged back upstairs.

In the morning Mom told me, "You know, after you left I got to thinking about it and I did buzz."

"I already know that, Mom."

"But you don't know why."

"No, I don't . . . and I'm not sure I want to!"

"Well," she grinned, "I dreamed I was peeling carrots and the buzzer was in my hand and I guess I pushed it as a knife. I'm really sorry."

What could I do but laugh at the whole silly situation?

Moving

When our family was faced with the question of what to do about my parents, it was not an easy decision and we could never have anticipated what lay ahead.

Earlier we had moved Mom and Dad from their Leisure World apartment into an apartment in a retirement home where Mom was no longer responsible for meals or housework. Then Dad, eighty-six years old at the time, suffered a stroke, and developed heart problems and severe back pain. Mom, because of her age, was unable to provide the necessary care, so after Dad spent some time in an acute-care hospital we moved him to a convalescent hospital.

Both Mom and Dad were unhappy with that arrangement. Mom did not drive so it meant we had to transport her to and from the facility. Dad's care was not what we had hoped for and we decided that I would take a six-month leave of absence from my position with the Orange County Department of Social Welfare to care for him. The plan entailed moving both Mom and Dad into our home where we would try home care. If able to cope, I'd resign my position and become a full-time nurse.

In the planning process, unforeseen problems rose like demons in our path. Our home had many steps and, to our horror, the bathroom doors were not wide enough to facilitate a wheelchair (a fact we'd never considered before). Thus the change became major: a new home.

However, moving had been part of our lifestyle so the detail of another move did not traumatize us. We located a house that would fit our needs, opened escrow, and put our present home on the market.

During the period of our decision making Dad was hospitalized again because of chest pains.

A Memorable Day

The day my leave began, Don and I closed escrow on our new house, and my sister and I took Mom over to her apartment from another hospital where she had undergone cataract surgery. Then I took my sister to the train depot to send her home, and went back to Mom's apartment to start my new position as a full-time nurse.

That evening, just after we'd turned the lights out, the phone rang. It was my husband, Don. "Dr. Harper just called," he reported. "When the floor nurse made her rounds she found your Dad had passed away in his sleep." All this in one day!

At the time I questioned God's wisdom. Why would God allow us to buy a new house and go through all the changes when He knew He was calling Dad home? But we went ahead with the plans, set up the two chosen rooms in the new house as Mom's small apartment and decided that Mom and I would relax and enjoy the six months before I returned to work.

Mom's Home Care

But to doubt God is foolish. Two months later, Mom had a major stroke. Because of our change in dwellings, our in-home facility was ready for this unexpected patient and, upon Mom's release from the hospital, my career as a "home-care nurse" began in earnest.

It was not a simple chore. Mom's left side was paralyzed and I had to learn many nursing skills. There were times when I considered running away.

The Visiting Nurse Association sent a nurse who arrived shortly after the ambulance brought Mother home.

The nurse's first questions to me were, "Can you move her from her bed to the wheelchair? Can you then get her to the bathroom?"

I replied with a frightened "No!" and wondered if our doctor had not been right when he said, "You shouldn't try to take her home. In her present condition, you can't give her the care she needs." But we had been through the convalescent hospital routine with Dad and I knew she wouldn't get the TLC there that we could give her.

The nurse continued, "Now, Mrs. Marvin, I'm going to show you how you can help Dorothea despite your paralysis. You've got to help her if she's going to be able to care for you."

I think she scared us both into concentrating and learning. "Dorothea, help her sit up and swing her feet off the bed. OK, Mrs. Marvin, now put your good right arm around her neck. Notice, both of you, that I have the wheelchair locked into the correct position."

Her next instruction was directed to me: "Hang on to her left side; put your feet against her feet so they won't slide; then pivot her into the chair." It was fantastic! I wheeled her into the bathroom and in the same manner pivoted her onto the toilet. We both giggled like a couple of kids because we knew we would make it.

The tub in her bathroom had a shelf at the back of it that was the same width and height as the tub. When the therapy sessions had strengthened her enough, I was able to get her backed up to that shelf, sit her down and swing her feet into the tub. In that way baths seemed real. Her feet were in water and I dribbled more water over her body.

I wish Florine DuFresne's excellent book, *Home Care*, had been available when I needed the help. It explains:

> An unexpected illness has left someone you love seriously disabled and in need of nursing care. Desiring to do your best to insure his comfort and well being, you are faced with an important decision. Is an extended care facility the best solution, or can you adequately care for your loved one at home?

An increasing number of families are unwilling to leave the responsibility of care to nursing homes. Gradually we are returning to a widening of the family circle to make room for the aged and ill, and to welcome them into a warm and supportive community of love.[2]

Home care can be managed if that is your decision. DuFresne's book gives step-by-step details on how to change your home into a care facility.

Rehabilitation was our next step. We were fortunate that the Easter Seal Rehabilitation Center was located in our city and I drove Mom there twice a week for therapy. Getting her in and out of the car was managed in the same way as moving her from the bed to the wheelchair. At that point Mom was three inches taller than I and about fifty pounds heavier but even the doctor became convinced that we had made the right decision.

By this time I had formally retired from my job because I knew Mom's care would be long term.

Privileges

It is unfortunate that in today's society many families no longer consider the extended family as a viable route. In many instances both parents are working and there is no one at home to care for an elderly or infirmed person. When I was a child, my grandmother lived with us for many years and was delightful company. I have nothing but good memories of her companionship and conversations. Our children of today miss a lot if they know nothing of the extended family concept.

Madeline L'Engle speaks of watching her grandchild, Lena, sitting at her great-grandmother's feet and reading to her from a nursery rhyme book that was upside down in her lap.[3] For children to have the privilege of knowing the elderly is special. Our sons have fond memories of all their grandparents, but especially Mom since she lived with us for more than four years.

6. HOSPICE CARE:

A service for the terminally ill—a team approach that

helps the family become a unit of care for a dying member. In some areas there are hospice (live-in) care units, but more frequently they are hospice *help* units organized to aid and support the caretaker.

The last thing anyone wants for the elderly or infirmed is unnecessary suffering and it may be that as you check out the available convalescent hospitals, you will decide none of them meet your needs. If that is the case, hospice might be the answer for you. Home Health Network, a part of the St. Joseph Hospital System in Orange County, California, has a hospice program as one branch of service offered. "Hospice is a philosophy of care that provides for the physical, psychological and spiritual needs of the terminally ill patient and family in the final stages of life."[4]

Because the hospice program is for the dying rather than those who will recover, it differs vastly from traditional health care. When hospice enters the picture the whole approach changes; there is no longer a denial of death. Their goal is to help the patient use his physical abilities as fully as possible, as long as possible.

Family Care

Hospice treats the family and the patient as a single unit with an emphasis on quality care for the remaining life of the patient. They use all available means to alleviate pain, anxiety and loneliness, including music, drama and recreational therapy. Most hospice programs encourage the family to be open in spiritual matters.

The emphasis is on dying at home if possible with the caretaker supported by a home-care team and twenty-four-hour, seven-day-per-week staff availability. Hospice groups have proven that the "care at home" concept draws families closer and helps friends and relatives become less fearful of the thought of someday having to face their own death.

The kindness and caring does not end at the death of the patient. Hospice workers give continued support to the family through their bereavement.

According to Schaeffer and Koop in *Whatever Happened*

to the Human Race?, those who stand on the principle that all of life is worth saving are reminded that there is a moral obligation involved with that stance. They need to activate a responsibility toward the dying aged and patients with terminal illnesses.

At most hospices, three things are done. First, all possible medical knowledge is employed to keep pain under control. Second, patients are visited, read to, and kept in almost constant contact with a loving human being, so they are not alone and deserted in that time when, of all times, being human means not being deserted. Third, families are treated as units; the family and its needs and the individual and his need are kept together as a human unit. These hospices are not in the business of dying, but of *living* right up to the end. Is this not the natural and rightful outflow of what we Christians believe about the abnormality of death and about the future resurrection victory we will experience through Christ?[5]

A story from St. Joseph Hospital's *Hospice Volunteer Voices* shares a first-hand case of how hospice works:

Christine and her mother, Joanne, had spent most of the weekend crying. The two women had come to one of the most difficult decisions they would ever make. Joanne would die at home, a victim of cancer.

"The doctors tell us she has six months at the longest," Christine told the social worker outside her mother's room. "They say chemotherapy and radiation may only give her another few months. Mom is sure she'd rather not have to deal with the time it would take and the side effects. She wants to die at home, but we're all alone. I'd like her to be home, too, but I don't know how to handle it," she cried.

The social worker helped Christine communicate her mother's wishes to the doctors and assisted with plans to move Joanne to more comfortable surroundings at home. Meanwhile Christine was introduced to St. Joseph Hospital's Home Health Hospice, to the people who would make it possible for her mother to be cared for in the home environment.

The Hospice nurse would supervise Joanne's medical care; she would help by assessing the necessary amount of pain medication needed to keep Joanne comfortable.

The nurse would also be responsible for reporting on Joanne's medical condition to the physician, and at regular Home Health Hospice Team meetings. The Home Health Aide would see Joanne three times a week, to bathe her and assist in personal care. Knowing her mother's immediate medical needs would be taken care of, Christine was anxious to have her mother come home. But, with the impending move home, came doubts and concerns about her ability to deal with her mother's illness . . . and how would they pay for all the services needed? Upon evaluation by the social worker, it was determined that "Light Up A Life" funds could help.* Christine was relieved; she knew she could contribute to the physical work that would have to be done, but now what of her mother's emotional needs? Would she know how to discuss her mother's death with her? With whom could Christine share her most intimate thoughts and concerns about losing her mother? The St. Joseph Hospice volunteer put her fears to rest.

The day Joanne was to leave the hospital, Vickie, the Hospice Volunteer, introduced herself to Christine. "I know you have a lot on your mind today," she said, "but I just wanted to let you know that I'll be available to help out; to spend some time with your mother, or to just listen. I'll let you decide how you'd like me to fit in. Should I give you a call in a few days after you and your mother have gotten settled at home?"

"I'll look forward to it," Christine said as she walked to her mother's room.

Those first few days were hectic, but Joanne was comfortable. The St. Joseph Hospital Home Health nurse had helped make the move easier. She familiarized Christine and her mother with the medical care that was needed. She also left her phone number in case of any medical emergency, and a schedule of her planned visits to the house during the first month.

The Home Health aide was introduced that first day, and made a visit to care for Joanne. When the phone

---

* The St. Joseph Hospital Home Health Network's "Light Up a Life" Hospice group has an annual fund raiser at the holiday season. Invitations are sent out for people to purchase a "light" for $10 in memory of or in honor of someone. They have a tree-lighting ceremony and the funds are used to assist families like the one in this story.

rang, Christine was glad to hear Vickie, the Hospice volunteer, on the other end.

"I hope it's not a bother," Vickie said, "but I've been thinking about you since meeting you at the hospital. I'd be glad to come out and see you and meet your mother whenever you'd like."

Christine told her a visit would be fine, and arranged for Vickie to come on Tuesday of the following week. "That way we'll be a little better situated," Christine said.

After Vickie's first few visits to the home, Christine and Joanne realized what an important part the Hospice volunteer was to St. Joseph's Home Health Hospice team. Vickie visited regularly, and was willing to talk with Joanne about her death whenever Joanne raised the subject. Sometimes Christine would join the conversations. Other times, she appreciated the chance to do things for herself while Vickie was with her mother. Joanne, Christine and Vickie became close friends during the three months before Joanne's death. As Joanne became weaker she spoke of her spiritual concerns. Christine mentioned this on a visit from the Home Health nurse, who was able to arrange several visits to the home by the Hospice chaplain. Joanne died comfortably and peacefully at home.[6]

Being Prepared

To be realistic, one person alone cannot adequately care for the needs of a terminally ill person. Hospice helps supply the necessary skills.

In the January 1986 issue of *Guideposts*, a heart-warming story is told of Jarrod, a young boy with an incurable disease, and the excellent care he received through a hospice program in Montana.

The hospice volunteer talked with him about his impending death and made him comfortable in facing the fact. When Jarrod spoke of being sick of his illness, the volunteer in a quiet, understanding tone told him, "My sister was paralyzed and she had a lot of pain. But right at the end, when I was holding her hand, I saw her smile."[7]

It is through sharing one's sadness with others that

healing begins. This is one of the outstanding features of hospice programs all around the country. Hospice volunteers are people who care.

When I read those stories, I thought, *Why didn't they have hospice programs when I was caring for Mom? Then she, too, could have died at home.*

The important thing in facing death is to be prepared — which is not an easy task, but a necessary one.

Recently our middle son and his family came for a visit because of the impending death of his father-in-law. The patient had been disabled for years and cancer recently had been discovered. When the latest malignancy appeared, he told his family he was ready to be with the Lord and wanted no heroic measures.

Our son asked me what our decision would be in a like situation. We informed him that we had both signed Durable Power of Attorney for Health Care forms (see chapter 11) and there would be no decisions regarding life support for any of our sons to make. Our wishes are set, even to the disposal of our mortal bodies (i.e., organ donation and burial or cremation), the services, memorial or otherwise, and all other incidentals that might arise. We also explained that his brothers were aware of and agreed with our wishes. He was relieved to know we are prepared.

The elderly population of our nation will increase from 6.8 percent in 1940 to an estimated 17 percent by 2020. The need for alternate care options is part of the planning that *must* be considered by our society, churches and individuals. But are we as individuals or are we as "the church" doing what we should in areas of concern for the elderly, the ill, the disabled and/or the dying?

8 | Individual and Group Support

> *O Lord, hear me praying; listen to my plea, O God my King, for I will never pray to anyone but you. Each morning I will look to you in heaven and lay my requests before you, praying earnestly* (Psalm 5:1-3, TLB).

IN HIS *Democracy in America*, Alexis de Tocqueville wrote:

These Americans are the most peculiar people in the world. You'll not believe me when I tell you how they behave. In a local community in their country, a citizen may conceive of some need which is not being met. What does he do? He goes across the street and discusses it with a neighbor. Then what happens? A committee comes into existence and the committee begins functioning in behalf of that need.[1]

Although written over a hundred years ago, he describes the methods still used to form many of the groups which produce "caring" organizations for the betterment of our world.

Jesus said, "For where two or three are gathered together in my name, there am I in the midst of them" (Matthew 18:20, KJV). And when we have Jesus as a partner, we can't go wrong. Therefore, as individual believers and as courageous church members, we need to study the issues that face our world today in the health care arena, and then step out and make our voices heard. We need to take a stand and support and help the people facing these dilemmas.

Handling the Feelings

In a recent issue of *Modern Maturity*, Nancy Badgwell, Ph.D., discussed the feelings some have when a parent or loved one is placed in a care facility.

> You hesitate, panic and agonize. Why? Because you feel guilty.
> Maybe these guilt feelings go back to your childhood. When we were children we were not to be angry. To be angry meant we were bad children. So, many of us turned our anger inward, becoming sad, joyless and sometimes guilty grownups.

Healthy Anger

Badgwell also points out that to feel angry is both normal and healthy.[2]

Guilt and anger are both party to the terminal care dilemma. It would be foolish to attempt to bury the reactions. They should be brought out into the open so they can be worked through.

These factors could be the focal point of a support group within a church. Wasn't Jesus angry when He overturned the money-changers' tables? If you deal with anger constructively, it can be healthy.

One has to think about guilt and fear also. A doctor told me, "The reason you could not sit and watch your mother die, and instead felt the need to call the paramedics, was that you felt guilty."

"Perhaps you are right," I replied, "but my recollection is that I feared she might be suffering."

"Not if she was comatose," he assured me. "When comatose, one feels no pain."

Had I known that, I might have been able to sit quietly by and wait for her to die. I don't know. Few of us know what we'll do in a given situation until we are there.

Badgwell goes on to quote from *The 36-Hour Day*, where Nancy L. Mace and Peter V. Rabins, M.D., discuss the fact that when feelings of guilt are not recognized they can warp our decision-making process. "The first step is to admit that feelings of guilt are a problem. They become a problem when they affect your decision."[3] Life-or-death decisions are difficult enough without guilt entering the situation, too.

Lennie-Marie P. Tolliver, Ph.D., former commissioner of the U.S. Administration on Aging, feels "family members need to recognize the fact that it's normal to have ambivalent feelings about placement."[4]

I absolutely agree. In pondering these facts and ideas, the word *vulnerable* popped into my mind. Webster defines vulnerable as "capable of being wounded; open to attack or damage."

Individual Efforts

Is vulnerability, perhaps, one reason more Christians do not become actively involved in support systems for the caretaker, care homes, grief ministries, hospice helpers and other areas of need?

Where have we gone astray? Jesus' admonition was: "Feed my sheep . . . and love one another" (see John 21:17 and 15:12, KJV). As Christians we are called to reach out and care for people. It is often our feeling of personal inadequacy that keeps us from following Jesus' admonition. We feel uncomfortable, unable to "jump in" and do our best even though we're not perfect.

Mother Teresa, known for her work with the indigent in India and elsewhere, is the best example of a caring person that I can think of, but we don't have to consider going out to the highways and byways of the world to care for those in need. We can become involved within our own neighborhood and church. Discover people with whom you can share tender loving care.

Jesus said, "I was sick and you visited me" (Matthew

25:36*b*, RSV). In caring for the infirmed we are often caring for someone who can give nothing in return; that is the kind of caring Jesus asks of us.

In *Whatever Happened to the Human Race?*, the authors affirm the importance of such one-to-one concern:

> Our concern is more than *not killing* the elderly and the ill. *It is giving them real life.* We must be realistic. This will cost each of us some of our personal peace and affluence. But we must do them — first of all because they are right. This is taught in the whole of the Bible. And second, it will be sharing the burdens of life, and one day it will be *our* turn to be helped — and we will be glad when we are.[5]

Where are the willing servants? Where are those who will serve the elderly and the infirmed with love? Early in February of 1987, I attended an all-day denominational church meeting where an award was presented to Nancy Fontaine for her work as activities director at the Hy-lond Convalescent Hospital in Westminster, California. Fontaine had organized a prayer vigil where the residents (she does not allow anyone to call them patients) at Hy-lond prayed for the seven U.S. hostages on a daily basis. Dr. Benjamin Weir, a former hostage, one of those for whom they prayed, was the guest speaker. He personally thanked her for the project, and them for their prayers. It was an emotional service.

I later visited the Hy-lond facility and talked with Fontaine about her work. When I returned I told my husband, "If you ever have to send me to such a facility, please send me there!" It is an example of what one loving person can do in the name of the Lord.

By law, facilities are required to have a director of activities. But Fontaine is more than that; she has found a way to return many of the residents to the world.

Fontaine's main thrust is to love and be a servant to everyone from every faith. Her recipe for life is to live it with love. It is her love that has changed fearful residents who were afraid to leave their rooms into outgoing and happy human beings. Her devotion to the facility and the residents goes above and beyond the usual activity director concept. She is a perfect example of *agape* love — the only way to love the "different" person.

As I visited with her, a woman approached in a wheel-chair. Fontaine called for her to come and meet me. She then explained, "Elsie has Alzheimer's and is very mixed up."

Elsie wheeled over and said, "Hello, but you are having a meeting. I won't bother you."

Nancy encouraged her by saying, "We are delighted to talk with you, Elsie — stop and visit awhile."

"No, I have things to attend to," Elsie replied. Then she looked at me and asked, "You will be back tomorrow, won't you, for the . . . " and her mind went no further.

"Of course I will," I reassured her.

She smiled as she wheeled away and said, "OK, don't forget now."

I grinned at Fontaine and replied, "Oh, I won't . . . I promise!"

Just to make this dear woman feel a part of our world for that short time was rewarding to me. The mixed-up aged are often shunned and put in a corner somewhere — but not if Nancy Fontaine is around.

She gave me a copy of a letter she had seen, the letter that had moved her into this work:

> *Hello! Is there anyone out there who will listen? How can I convince you that I am a prisoner? For five years I have not seen a park or the ocean or even a few feet of grass.*
>
> *I'm an 84-year-old woman and the only crime I've committed is to have an illness which is considered chronic. I needed help to stay in my home, but there was no one. So I wound up in a convalescent hospital.*
>
> *All kinds of people are here. I sit and watch day after day. I see pathetic ones (maybe the lucky ones) who have lost their minds and the poor souls who shouldn't be here but nobody comes to get them, the sick ones who are in pain . . . and we're all locked up here together.*
>
> *I keep in touch with the world through the newspaper,*

reading about Medicare changes, but all I can see is that nurses spend more time writing. For how do you regulate caring?

A doctor comes to see me once a month and spends approximately three to five seconds and a few more minutes writing in the chart or joking with the nurses. (My doctor doesn't come to convalescent hospitals so I had to take this one.) I wonder how the aides feel when they work so hard for so little pay and see the person who spends so little time making the most money?

No one checks to see if my nails are trimmed or body really clean. Baths often are missed but if I complain they'd say she doesn't remember . . . and I'd be labeled a complainer.

I remember how I used to cook and bake. Here I have no choice of what or when I eat. It's been so long since I've eaten any fresh fruit!

As I write this I wish I were exaggerating. These last five years seem like five hundred. I'm writing this because many of you may live to be old like me and by then it will be too late. You, too, will be stuck here and wonder: Is there no justice in life? Right now, I pray every night that I may die in my sleep and get this nightmare called life over with.

This human tragedy is a truism for many of the homes to which we send our elderly and infirmed. And it is up to concerned individuals to improve their lot.

Nancy Fontaine reached out and found support from the community. "Most important," she claims, "is the residents' *need* for love. You have to find people who really love older folks—individuals who have empathy and compassion. It is elevating to put oneself in the position of servant. It's a case of giving people like these, who do not have control of their lives, an identity and an opportunity for decision making. It gives them life.

"Once you are a resident of one of these facilities everything is regulated. You eat what and when they say; the lights go out at a certain time; you get up at a specified time. Even if a person is alert and healthy he seldom feels free to express his feelings."

Fontaine paused, then continued, "And if a person is already passive, his spirit is held down because he has no say in his daily activities. Now we have meetings where the residents discuss feelings, become vocal and make decisions."

"If I wanted to start a work like this somewhere," I asked, "how would I go about helping residents come alive again? How did you accomplish these changes?"

"It's easy," she replied. "Just give them decision-making opportunities and let *yourself* become the servant. How would you feel if I put you in the sun and then left you, or suddenly pulled your chair sideways without telling you where you were going, or pushed you up to a table and said, 'Here is your food. Now eat it all'? That is treating them like children and they've been there once. They need to be treated like adults . . . so I repeat: The most important part is for you to become the servant. If you want to move them, ask them first if they'd like to sit in the sun. Just treat them as you'd like to be treated."

We need more Nancy Fontaines, people who are willing to serve with love and to organize activities to keep our elderly from wasting away in unhappy circumstances.

Christian Influence

In Minnesota's Twin Cities a peer counseling program has been developed within the Presbytery of that area. It is based on a counseling project begun seven years ago at the University of Minnesota with a National Institutes of Mental Health grant.

The decision was reached to utilize older adults' abilities . . . abilities gained from life-long experiences. Although based on the university's training manual, the counseling program was developed with the use of Christian literature, Scripture and prayer. The counselors, also called Christian Caregivers, developed listening skills. They are aware that clergy, often too busy to really listen, may give the person an answer rather than discuss the problem and allow the person to reach his own decision.

These counselors have time and are trained to ask,

"What is the problem?" They then help the person reach a decision which is workable for that person.

Grief Ministry

Individually and collectively, we need to reach out and touch the suffering, the dying, the caretakers—*and* the grieving.

Recently a friend of mine visited a support group for widows. She told of how one member described the experience of many when she stated, "Actually my period of grieving began when my husband was first moved to a care facility. That was the point when, in my mind, I felt he had really died."

We need caring people to form "Grief and Helping Ministries" within our churches, to reach out to families who grieve over the death or impending death of loved ones. When death does occur, the church needs to be keenly aware of the feelings those left behind will have and then be ready and able to lend support.

In *The Healing Power of Grief*, Jack Silvey Miller tells of discovering "the reason for and importance of funeral and memorial services."[6] After presiding at the funeral of a child of dear friends, he realized:

> He [God] doesn't will that we should suffer, but in our suffering He cares for us and wants to get near us. If we're open, He will come, even in the darkest night, and stand with us. He lost a son, too.
> Theologically, that makes good sense. It is the very purpose and plan of the cross of Christianity, that God can identify with the very worst of the human condition. Death. And the rest of the story is the very hope of life — that we were not born for the grave.[7]

As family, friends, and fellow church members, we should speak to the bereaved about their loved one. We all will, or all have, faced the death of a loved one and that person's memory should not be buried with the body. If the members of the family want to talk, then talk, and share the good times you remember, and laugh with them. It may comfort them to reminisce about those happy times.

These excerpts from a letter written by a bereaved man to a family traveling the road he had traveled help us understand how the bereaved feel. Keep these thoughts in mind when you minister to others.

> Be patient with your friends. There is no way for them to imagine the pain you are feeling. Most people think of death and all its aspects only when it touches them personally.
>
> I learned quickly which people could accept me as a heartbroken, grieving person. I could draw strength from them. Others, I found, needed me to be strong. They could draw strength from me. Both were, and still are, very necessary in my life.
>
> I have tried to be honest. There were times I wanted to die. I repeatedly asked God why He took the two people in the world who knew how to live — who loved life more than any I have ever known. He never told me because *He didn't take them — He received them when they came.*[8]

One person alone can start the process of making changes, but it takes a caring community to continue it. Our churches must work in this area, because the real need is love . . . and isn't that what Christianity is all about?

9 The Role
of the Church

> *Let us not love with words or tongue but with actions and*
> *in truth (1 John 3:18,* NIV).

THE CHRISTIAN LEADERS I questioned all felt
strongly that the church must be available to help families
make decisions regarding the care of their terminally ill
loved ones. Here is how those leaders expressed their feelings:

Are there situations in which the church should enter
the picture?

PASTOR A:
Yes, the church should become involved in at least two
ways. First, in clarifying biblical teaching. Interestingly
enough, in both the miraculous healing of Hezekiah from
a terminal illness [2 Kings 20:1-7] and the resurrection
of Lazarus [John 11:1-44; 12:1,2], the patients enjoyed a
resumption of a conscious, meaningful life — Hezekiah
for more than fifteen years! Second, churches can aid in
the support and counsel of people facing these difficult
decisions.

THEOLOGIAN:
We have an obligation to provide moral directives
which are biblically grounded. The difficulty is that often
you do not have an explicit biblical mandate but you try
to extrapolate what you do from a biblical principle. Then

the question arises, How far do you extrapolate and at what point does the extrapolation become so tenuous as to be merely a matter of preference or opinion? That's where the difficulty arises and varying opinions develop. That life is precious in the sight of God, that life is to be protected and enhanced – those principles are biblical. But when it comes to specific cases we may find genuine differences of opinion among equally obedient disciples of Christ, precisely because we do not have specific directives covering the problems created by modern medical technology. I think that, if necessary, we must err on the side of valuing and preserving life.

PASTOR B:

Yes, there are times when the church should enter the picture. Primarily the church should come along when invited by the patient and/or family or, for that matter, by the doctor. The church may serve as a "go-between" in the negotiating process. For example, the church may get involved by helping with financial considerations. The greatest contribution, however, will be in the spiritual realm, offering prayer, undergirding, giving emotional support, etc.

PASTOR C:

The church must enter the picture. I believe it already has. Let me quote from the Presbyterian Form of Government [G-1.0300]:

> 3. The Historic Principles of Church Order: In setting forth the following form of government, discipline, and service, the Presbyterian Church (U.S.A.) reaffirms the historic principles of church order which have been part of our common heritage in this nation and which are basic to our Presbyterian concept and system of church government, namely: (1) That "God alone is Lord of the conscience, and hath left it free from the doctrines and commandments of men which are in anything contrary to his word, or beside it, in matters of faith or worship."

Therefore, we consider the rights of private judgement, in all matters that respect religion, as universal and unalienable: we do not even wish to see any religious constitution aided by the civil power, further than may be necessary for protection and security, and at the same time, be equal and common to others.

PASTOR D:

We enter the picture in response to the needs and requests for help from family members. It is not our role to try to make such important decisions for other people, but to serve as resources for needed ethical and spiritual guidance.

PRIEST:

The churches and parishes can be involved at various levels of education and should support the patient as well as the family. For example, one difficult aspect of an illness is the social isolation that sickness brings. The parish community, represented by small groups who visit the sick and pray for them, can serve both patient and family by providing personal presence and care, communicating acceptance and belonging even in the isolation. This kind of companioning can help both the patient and family bear whatever suffering and tragedy might accompany the illness.

This is one of the most effective ways a church can enter the picture in life-support decisions. Form a group and train them to become listeners and caregivers. All need to face the prospect of death while keeping an open mind about the pros and cons of medical marvels. Our church groups need to discuss the facts involved, to study Scripture and to pray for the correct answers . . . then listen for God's reply. We must openly discuss the risks involved in relaxing the laws about allowing death. We do not want to run the risk of another holocaust, but on the other hand, there is a need to educate the world and inform people of the promised peace and beauty of life in the hereafter.

Church Support Groups

Many churches already have groups that help those in need. I found one in the Fletcher Hills area of El Cajon, California, that could be used as a model. Their program offers free respite care by trained volunteers and is available to any area resident in need. Developed by Dorothy Moses, MS, RN, a former professor at San Diego State University and a gerontological consultant, the program is part of the senior adult ministry in the Fletcher Hills Presbyterian Church. From a humble beginning of serving their own church members, the group has become non-denominational, trains volunteers from all walks of life, and helps *anyone* in need regardless of their beliefs.

"Just what does the respite care program do?" I asked Ms. Moses.

"You name it, we do it," she laughed. "Seriously, our respite care program is focused on the totally disabled person who is being cared for at home by a family member. We do help some people who live alone but most of our clients are elderly couples. Many times the person providing the care has chronic disabilities to the point where I wonder sometimes which one is the most disabled. A definition is: the temporary supervision of a dependent person with the intention of giving the primary caregiver some free time."

"What a wonderful help you provide," I replied. "I was physically able to care for my mother, but it would have been marvelous to have been relieved once in awhile. For the elderly couple your workers must appear as angels. Are the helpers young?"

"My volunteers are of all ages, but mostly retired people plus a few young mothers. The clients we serve have total chronic disabilities such as Alzheimer's disease, post stroke with unresolved paralysis, Parkinson's disease; and we have some terminal cancer patients."

"Do you provide nursing type care?"

"No, it does not involve homemaking or nursing care. A common example would be a situation where a volunteer couple goes out together; one stays with the patient, while the other takes the caregiver to a doctor's appointment, shopping or whatever the needs."

"Are these services free?"

"Yes. We decided we didn't want to become involved in 'grant' money. The church has put some money into our budget. Each volunteer is given little cards we made up that ask for donations to the church if a person can afford it. It is strictly volunteer giving and money does come in." (Information on how to form a care group such as this one in your area can be obtained by writing the Fletcher Hills

Presbyterian Church. See appendix A for the address.)

"Sunshine Visitation"

Another helping group in the Southern California area started with an organization called Sunshine Visitation. Their main focus is having a one-on-one contact with a single person in need.

Joan Keefe, director of senior adult ministries in the Solana Beach Presbyterian Church, explained, "The group is primarily made up of young mothers with children still at home who wanted to do something for others. They weren't ready to become deacons, so we set up this program to tie people together. For example, one volunteer picks up two women every Thursday and takes them grocery shopping. They have 'adopted' her baby as their grandchild.

"We have several young couples who have adopted a grandparent. Older people need children, not on a 24-hour basis but occasionally. It is a rule that they are not to be asked to babysit. This isn't a program to help the young people, but for those young people to help the aged.

"We also have another group, a 'Program of Enablers' which was originally Presbyterian-centered and involved sixteen churches in the San Diego area. However, the program has become ecumenical. We're now helping other denominations train lay people for older adult ministry in areas such as grief recovery and pre-retirement, and to point out the importance of specific intentional ministry to older adults."

"That sounds excellent," I interjected.

"We believed we had something going for us and felt the need to share what we had learned. The ecumenical outreach has just begun. In fact, it's interesting to note that ministry with older adults is moving into the seminary level as well.

"Many churches use the able-bodied older adult to visit the adult who is a no-go. One of my neighbors coined the phrase: 'the go-go's, the slo-go's and the no-go's.' In that way we cover the whole spectrum of the aging."

"Do you have single and divorcee volunteers in both programs?" I asked.

"Yes, the divorced often come in and say, 'Help, I need an older person to talk to . . . to benefit from their wisdom.'"

Action Needed

History will show that the church was responsible for the care of the sick long before the government became involved. If the "church" is a "caring people," why aren't we developing more church-administered care facilities—facilities where the level of care is of more importance than making a profit? There are many areas in the care of the elderly and infirmed that the church needs to address. Two questions come to mind:

- What about the thousands of people who are refused medical care because they cannot afford it—and die as a result?
- Is such a refusal of care a form of national euthanasia?

The church, the body of Christ, needs to re-examine its actions. Are we being obedient? Proverbs warns us:

Wisdom cries aloud in the street: in the markets she raises her voice (1:20, RSV).

And you have ignored all my counsel and would have none of my reproof, I also will laugh at your calamity; I will mock when panic strikes you (1:25,26, RSV).

But he who listens to me will dwell secure and will be at ease, without dread of evil (1:33, RSV).

10 | Understanding Ethical/Medical/Legal Complexities

> *When the Holy Spirit, who is truth, comes, he shall guide you into all truth, for he will not be presenting his own ideas, but will be passing on to you what he has heard. He will tell you about the future* (John 16:13, TLB).

CAN CARING AND hurting overlap? In the case of Paul Brophy, they did. Our legal system caused unnecessary suffering for the Brophy family. After discovering an aneurysm early in 1983, Brophy's physicians informed him of the possible risks involved with the necessary neurosurgery. As a fireman he had seen many people in a comatose state, and prior to surgery he informed his family that if anything went wrong, he did not want to be kept alive on life-support systems.

He returned from the surgery speechless, immobile, incontinent, and totally unresponsive to smiles, speech or touch. His wife agreed to a feeding tube because she was assured it would make him more comfortable.

After about a year and a half, Mrs. Brophy, who is a nurse, realized her husband was not going to recover and asked for the feeding tube to be removed. She was informed that the action would cause the death of her husband and that her request had been denied. The case went to court.

After five months, the judge decided Paul Brophy's quality of life could not be considered. Since he was in a vegetative condition, he felt no discomfort. Therefore, the feeding tube was no burden to him. The judge further noted that it would violate medical ethics to remove the tube.

An historic Massachusetts Supreme Court decision was finally reached in 1986 which allowed the Brophy family to arrange for the removal of the feeding tube.

According to William F. Schulz, as quoted in *USA Today*, the issue raised these questions:

- What does it mean to be human?
- Is life simply a matter of flesh and breath?
- Or do we require thought, tears, light and love to claim true humanity?

He added, "The complexity of this case turns on a conflict between two moral standards: the state's obligation to defend the life of the innocent, and the Brophy family's to preserve their loved one's self-possession and integrity."[1]

When the tube was removed, Brophy died. One doctor stated that he could have lived another thirty-five years if the feeding tube had not been removed. Yet as Thomas Jefferson wrote, "Of all human complaints, the most abhorrent is the body without mind."

A Continuing Conflict

For the doctor it is often the fear of professional failure that pushes him to continue life-sustaining measures. If there is no chance for survival, is that the proper decision?

The conflict continues. Some right-to-life groups claim that food and water are ordinary care, not extraordinary. Once the feeding tube is in place it requires only nursing maintenance, causes no discomfort and removal would cause death by dehydration and starvation.

Kathryn Lindskoog, in *C.S. Lewis, Mere Christian*, highlights an interesting comment: "One April day in his twenty-fourth year, when he was a student at Oxford, C. S. Lewis wrote in his journal: 'I wish life and death were not the only alternatives, for I don't like either.' "[2]

At another time Lewis stated: "There are, aren't there, only three things we can do about death: to desire it, to fear it, or to ignore it?"[3]

No one can ignore death; many fear it; and some desire it.

At a medical conference a speaker quoted Robert Barry, a Dominican priest, who had written the following: "I hold that nutritional fluids are aspects of normal care and are to be provided to all patients — even the terminally ill — until certain determination of death has been made."

Many people agree with this concept, and many do not. Again, it is a gray area with no definitives. It becomes a moral issue of whether food is considered ordinary or extraordinary. Does the caretaker murder the person by removing food or does he simply allow nature to release the person to an unassisted death?

The Medical/Moral/Judicial Tangle

In 1983 the President's Commission for the Study of Ethical Problems in Medicine and Biomedical and Behavioral Research completed an exhaustive study entitled: *Deciding to Forego Life-Sustaining Treatment.*[4] It covers ethical, medical and legal issues in treatment. The study addresses the complex issues, and the resulting report is easy to read as well as enlightening for the non-medically trained reader.

The report asserts: "The voluntary choice of a competent and informed patient should determine whether or not life-sustaining therapy will be undertaken." It further states that the health care institution and the doctor should help the patient form his own opinion by explaining the various types of treatment available.

The Commission recommends: "Serve patients best by maintaining a presumption in favor of sustaining life, while recognizing that competent patients are entitled to choose to forego treatments."

The health care professional must also protect the patient who is unable to reach a decision for himself; in

such cases, the report suggests that a surrogate be named
to help.

The report includes a discussion on CPR (cardiopulmonary resuscitation). From my interviews I learned that
watching a loved one being "paddled" back to life by an
electrical charge can be a horrible experience. Many of us
have watched the procedure on TV, and it is frightening.
The recommendation given is that if the procedure will not
benefit the patient, "a decision not to resuscitate, with the
consent of the patient or surrogate, is justified."

However, if the doctor disagrees, the Commission suggests further discussion or transfer to a different physician.
Judicial review is to be used as a last resort.

When the decision reaches a point between action or
omission of treatment, morals enter the picture.

> Whatever considerations justify not starting should
> justify stopping as well. Thus the Commission concludes
> that neither law nor public policy should mark a dif-
> ference in moral seriousness between stopping and not
> starting treatment.

One of many people who have faced this type of decision
is Paul Spitz, a Southern California pastor. He shared the
story of his wife's death with me. As a severe diabetic she
had been hospitalized for two and a half months because of
near kidney failure. Neither her stomach nor bladder func-
tioned and she also suffered congenital heart failure.
Although she was only thirty-nine, her poor vital signs
rated her physically like an eighty-year-old.

Her chest pain was so severe that the fifteen units of
Demerol she was given every three hours was increased to
125 units every ninety minutes. She existed for that shot.

"I couldn't get through to her spirit," Spitz stated. "She
was mellow . . . on a drug-induced high.

"When Jesus was on the cross, He said that He gave up
His Spirit. I believe one of the natural causes of death is
when a person, by an act of his own will, desires to give up
his life."

That concept had come to my mind on the night of my father's death. Mom had said, "He willed himself to die because he knew I would be taken care of by living with you." At the time I thought, *Sure, Mom, believe what you wish* . . . but maybe she had more insight into his death than I.

As I pulled my thoughts back to the interview, Spitz continued, "She was so drugged — an I.V. in her arm and an oxygen mask on her face. She was unable to think; she was not really a person. Her will was gone. The doctors gave her no more than a few days."

"Was she in the intensive care unit?" I asked.

"Yes, she had been for weeks. Her deterioration was so rapid it was scary. I fell apart, but I believed the doctor. We had prayed, fasted, anointed her and sought God's healing through all the years of her failing health; but the Bible says there is a point where man wants to die, and I believed this was happening.

"However, I wanted her to die at home, not in the confines of ICU hooked up to all that weird equipment. I found a nurse, removed the oxygen and the I.V. which was pumping twelve different medications into her, and we moved her home. She was unable even to keep water down, and when we gave her medication the first day, she threw it up, so we stopped that, too. At the time no one expected her to live. I just wanted her home, no longer being kept alive artificially.

"We monitored her diabetes carefully and gave her insulin injections every three hours, but no more morphine. I prayed that she might have a sound mind again, that I might have the godly woman I had married back with us before she died, to see her spirit come alive and allow God's mercy to come in."

Spitz put his hands over his face for a moment, then looked up. His face revealed the pain he had suffered.

"What an experience," I shuddered.

"It was, but it reinforced for me the need for people to face reality. And death is reality.

"She went into a coma that lasted three days, and on the day she woke up, God met her. She was again coherent. She had gone sixteen days without food, and for a diabetic that alone is a miracle. However, as I said, we had carefully monitored her blood sugar. We welcomed back our wife and mother and it was an extremely happy time. She was delighted to be a part of our family circle again.

"I truly believe our body puts itself into shock or trauma when we are overloaded with pain. She recovered despite the doctor's prognosis and we had a wonderful year, then two more while she again underwent dialysis . . . but they were good years, too."

"When did you lose her?" My voice was shaky with the emotion of his story.

"We had the three years and then she had a severe heart attack. She was hospitalized in the evening, and at 7 A.M. she died. But through CPR, they brought her back to life. I stood by and watched them use the paddles *eleven* times.

"At first, I was too emotionally involved to realize what this was doing to her. Finally, I came to my senses, and realized she was unable to ask them to stop. She couldn't talk but she'd squeeze my hand. 'Hey,' I said, 'this is enough! God is calling her home and you keep bringing her back . . . NO MORE! STOP!'

"And I have never regretted my decision. Oh, I've missed her, but to live as an invalid was not her desire."

Paul Spitz has since added the position of hospital chaplain to his vocations. I'm certain the experiences with his wife's illness and death make him special in the field.

The Doctor's Oath

From a medical standpoint, the doctor's loyalty to his Hippocratic oath sometimes comes into conflict with the patient's or his family's wishes. Here is how some of the Christian leaders felt about that:

Do you believe a patient's family's feelings about the use of life support should be considered before a doctor's Hippocratic oath?

PASTOR A:
I certainly do.

THEOLOGIAN:
I think that the ultimate focus of concern is the family and that the family in this case has to take priority. While the doctor must be faithful to his oath, he may feel he cannot work with a particular family. That can mean finding someone who would feel morally free, someone who, though bound by his oath, still could cooperate with the family in turning off some of the life-sustaining equipment.

PASTOR B:
I hate to see a patient's or family's feelings about life support contrasted with a doctor's Hippocratic oath obligations. I know it happens, and it is an indication of the complex times in which we live. When there is a conflict, there must be a time of mutual negotiation so that both doctor and family/patient are put in a win/win position. That may take creative negotiating and painful give and take, but it is the obligation that bridges any conflicting claims.

PASTOR D:
The patient, when fully conscious and responsible, is to determine treatment after being fully informed about his or her medical condition. If the patient is unconscious, then the family should decide on the treatment after being fully informed. It's difficult for me to imagine the wishes of a family conflicting with a physician's commitment to medical ethics or with the standards of the profession if the family is fully informed about the prognosis of a patient.

PRIEST:
The patient's and family's feelings and the doctor's commitment to "do no harm" ought not to be seen as exclusive alternatives. The patient's total good is the object of medical care. This includes both the patient's care and preference. Respecting these preferences is a way of respecting the moral worth of the patient. However, the physician also has moral integrity, and what the patient prefers may conflict with what the physician is morally able to supply. As an example, the patient may prefer a fatal injection but the physician may be morally unable

to cooperate. Any physician who is not able to serve the total good of a patient by cooperating with the patient's preference, and who is unable to persuade the patient to choose otherwise, ought to follow the standard procedure for withdrawing from the case.

Opinions on this subject vary, but not to a large degree, and some feel there should be no conflict at all.

After considering the facts and thoughts shared by these men of God, and others, regarding all these issues, what does one do? Just how does one go about making a decision?

11 | Decision Making

---

*For our earthly bodies, the ones we have now that can die,
must be transformed into heavenly bodies that cannot
perish but will live forever. When this happens, then at
last this Scripture will come true—"Death is swallowed
up in victory"* (1 Corinthians 15:53,54, TLB).

ARE THERE STEPS to follow in working out the
proper answer to a life-or-death decision? Not in the absolute sense, perhaps, but there are some guidelines that
will help. We will start with the legal area.

Legal Concerns

Courts are now strong on patient autonomy—the right
to make one's own decision. Therefore, hospitals today
should follow the patient's wishes concerning heroic
measures, but it does not always work out that way. This
is the reason documents have been developed to cover the
necessary details in case of a life-threatening situation.

There are a variety of forms; Durable Power of Attorney for Health Care, Physicians Directive, Natural Death
Act and Living Will are examples. They are called Personal
Preference Documents and have been mentioned several
times in the text. To sign such a form may seem unimpor-
tant, but it is signed to be certain your wishes are carried

out. It also relieves spouse or children, or whoever is designated as your health-care agent, from having to make the "tough" decisions if it becomes necessary.

Both my husband and I are senior citizens in good physical health, but tomorrow that could change. We each have filled out and signed a Durable Power of Attorney for Health Care form because that document is legal in the state of California. Other states have, or hopefully will develop, documents of this type. To find what is legal for your place of residence, check with your doctor, hospital or attorney. For those fortunate enough to have more than one home, be certain that what is signed is legal for each place of residence.

Because our youngest son lives near us, he is the person given first authority to act on our behalf.

When decision time comes and a patient is mentally incompetent, comatose, or otherwise incapable of reaching a decision, a surrogate should be named. But the documents should be signed *before* there is such a need, while one is mentally alert and not emotionally upset because of a serious illness. This will prevent unnecessary heartache.

An example of the importance of these documents appears in the January 1987 issue of *Readers Digest*. The daughter of a thoughtful gentleman who had looked ahead tells of his active life as a widower. He attended senior citizen meetings and the Retirees Club, and he "squired various widows around town." His independence and friendliness were a joy to everyone, including his family. You can feel the love that was shared as the story progresses.

The author goes on to explain: "One day, he brought me a piece of paper from the lawyer at the Senior Citizens Center. I didn't like it, but he made me take it and then said, 'Promise to bring it to me when I tell you.' "

He had not, however, taken proper care of his health. He had ignored early warning signs of cancer, and it reached an advanced stage. After several hospitalizations for surgery, deterioration accompanied his struggle to regain health and he was again hospitalized.The prognosis this time was poor. He said to his daughter, "Bring it to me." She knew he meant "that paper."

The "paper" was a type of living will. There were no decisions required by the family. The directive was a written request for no life-support measures. The article ends: "His decision was the last and best gift he gave to me. All my memories are good. He lived the way he wanted and died the way he chose."[1]

That man's family did not have to make any decision. They supported him through his first attempts to beat the cancer, then loved and continued to support him as he lived out his final wish—to die with no heroic measures being taken to save him.

One of the doctors I interviewed about this subject said, "When it comes to the elderly or the infirmed who do not want to be hooked up to these technical advances or who are unable to reach such a decision, I say, 'Let go and let God.' That may be a cop-out, but God *should* be in charge of this world and in many instances we are not allowing Him that opportunity. By the use of life support we may be overruling God's plan for the patient."

Yet there are different views. In chapter 4, I told you about Nancy, the wife of the young man injured in the car accident. Nancy still finds proof that, even in his comatose state, John ministers to others. There is no absolute answer.

A Caution

Although right-to-die forms such as we have signed are legal, opposition to the documents must be considered also.

When I told a doctor friend that Don and I had signed our "papers," he looked at me and said, "Do you know what you have signed?"

"Of course," I replied. "I wouldn't sign anything without reading and understanding it."

"Well," he smiled, "if you broke your hip tomorrow, do you realize a doctor might not be willing to pin it?"

"What? You've got to be kidding!"

"I'm not trying to be funny. You just told me you signed a paper that says *no* medical treatment is to be given to you."

"But, that's if I am terminal or suffering—not for a broken hip."

"Aha! That depends on the doctor—and on the interpretation of the document. You know, there are some children or spouses who could withhold treatment because of that paper if they wanted to get rid of you.

"I have an elderly patient right now who is mentally incapable of knowing what she wants. If her husband asked me to 'pull the plug,' I'd refuse. This is a second marriage. A few months ago she was a bright and articulate woman who handled all their finances because the money is hers. I would be fearful of assisting her death by withdrawal of any medical aids because of that situation. It isn't an easy position for a doctor."

That conversation made me stop and think. It might seem ridiculous for most families, but there are people who might do something frightful if a great deal of money were involved. In fact, this brings us into the area of "elder abuse," an area of which I had no former knowledge. *Modern Maturity* addressed the subject in an article entitled, "The Shame of Elder Abuse:"

> Shame: That's why they don't call for help, why they suffer the verbal abuse, the loss of freedom, even the beatings.
> Who would inflict such treatment on a defenseless person? In this case, the perpetrator is most likely a member of the victim's own family.
> How bad is it?
> Frequently quoted figures projected from 1980 reports of state protective service agencies suggest that one out of every 25, or about one million, older Americans are abused each year.
> Elder abuse falls into four categories: financial/material; psychological; physical; and neglect, divided into active neglect (where food, medication, etc.,

are deliberately withheld) and passive neglect (where a caregiver is unable — because of ignorance or inability — to meet the older person's needs).[2]

In the society in which we live, it is both frightening and disgusting to admit that such things happen. In a country like ours the situation is deplorable . . . but true. So you want to be absolutely certain of the trustworthiness of the person appointed to carry out your wishes. And, of course, a will or family trust must be available as well so there can be no errors about what is to be done with your assets.

A pamphlet put out by the Human Life Alliance of Minnesota, Inc., about living wills states:

> The Minnesota Legislature is again considering living will-type legislation. Although the form varies greatly, generally a "Living Will" is a declaration or directive instructing a physician to withhold or discontinue medical treatments from the signer if he/she is terminally ill and unable to make decisions.
>
> Promoted by "Dear Abby," pro-euthanasia (mercy killing) and "right to die" groups — and, increasingly in the popular media — many people have assumed that living wills are good and necessary tools to protect the rights of patients to make decisions at the end of their lives. They may be unaware that living wills and living will-type legislations are:
>
> UNNECESSARY
> COUNTERPRODUCTIVE
> DANGEROUS
>
> Most people are unaware that the "Living Will" is the brain child of the pro-euthanasia, pro-suicide movement.

The pamphlet further explains the meaning of several phrases which are often used in these types of documents.

> *Incurable or irreversible condition:* This includes asthma, diabetes, cerebral palsy, many conditions caused by heart or stroke, etc.
>
> *Death within a relatively short time:* This could be hours — or weeks or months.
>
> *No longer able to make decisions:* Could include those affected by medication, overwhelmed or depressed by

problems, mildly senile, etc. Note: No living will requires
that patients be notified of its going into effect.

Withhold or withdraw treatment: This could include
respirators or chemotherapy. But it could also include
medications upon which a patient is dependent (insulin,
nitroglycerin, blood pressure regulators) oxygen, antibiotics — even food and water.

My attending physician: Your family doctor and
friend? The specialist you've never really talked to? An
intern in an emergency room in a strange city?[3]

Thoughts to ponder! And I have pondered them. Our
decision still remains the same. Don and I have signed the
Durable Power of Attorney for Health Care forms and are
comfortable with our decision. We do *not* want our sons to
be saddled with any problems in case either of us is in that
type of situation. However, everyone will not agree with
our thinking on the matter.

In *Terminating Life*, Gary E. McCueb and Therese
Boucher state: "The crucial point is that certain conditions
will produce a death that is more comfortable, more pre-
dictable, and more permitting of a conscious and peaceful
experience than others."

The book continues: "When the alternatives are death
with dignity, or death accompanied by prolonged pain and
distress, common sense as well as compassion support our
demand that the choice should belong to the individual."[4]

Euthanasia is, of course, in direct opposition to the
Christian belief that all life is sacred, and I agree with the
right-to-lifers to this point. I could not have given my
mother pills or anything that would have killed her. But
compassion allowed me to refuse another session for her in
the acute-care hospital, with more I.V.'s, which at best
would have given Mother only another six months.

The Financial Dilemma

Another area of concern in the arena of health care is
the financial. Medicare and individual insurance coverages
are not enough when a long illness and/or many surgeries,
chemotherapy or other forms of treatment are necessary.
Extended periods of hospitalization can bankrupt a family.

Paul Brophy's care has been estimated at over $200 a day . . . multiplied by years.

When finance enters the picture it opens a whole new vista. It does cost a lot of money when someone becomes ill. Each test and surgical procedure is expensive, and the consensus varies on the importance of trying every means to maintain life. I asked the Christian leaders two more questions:

1. *How important are financial considerations?*

PASTOR A:
Finances from a practical point of view are important — very important. The all-important thing, however, is to realize that God's resources are not limited. He has promised to supply all our needs (Philippians 4:19). Whatever constitutes the medical attention needed in a given situation, we have His word on it — He will provide.

THEOLOGIAN:
Finances are important especially with the aged. Consider a couple in their seventies. If the husband is hospitalized, it may mean that, regardless of what the state provides, his wife is left absolutely destitute. I think the husband in that situation would say, "I want to terminate my life." Not by suicide but by refusing the expensive equipment that would only prolong his dying process. That kind of decision might well be made in love by a Christian husband.

Through all of this the big issue is: When does our utilization of modern medical technology become unnatural — prolonging life which, if nature per se were allowed to take its course, would quite speedily end? I do think we want to use all available resources to keep people free from pain. There comes a time, though, when some of us would prefer not to have the new techniques and equipment used, but to allow God to terminate our existence by letting nature run its course.

PASTOR B:
Financial considerations are important, but they are not a controlling factor. If there is hope, then the finances must be found. Perhaps more churches and/or church families should be tapped as a financial resource in such emergencies.

PASTOR C:
Financial considerations are important, and wise attorneys need to be consulted lest the situation be compounded even further. I happen to believe that, in a nation like ours, government should be involved. My personal bias is that we should weigh the support of medical costs against the astronomical expenditures we are making on weapons that will not only kill people but leave many on life-support systems or with such handicaps that life will hardly be worth living.

PASTOR D:
They are important in such matters but ought not to be made all-important.

PRIEST:
Financial considerations are always important since they express our sense of responsibility for our loved ones and society at large. However, they need not be the singular determining factor in a decision for treatment.

2. *What if someone came to you and said, "I've been asked to sell our home to support my spouse who is in a fetal position, totally oblivious to the world . . . or to divorce him." What would you recommend?*

PASTOR A:
To me that question is in two parts—and the first part needs to be answered in two parts. First, what decision has been made about the use of life-support systems? Only if they are to be used is the question relevant. If that is the decision, one should then ask, What other means of financing the costs are available? There may be several options. The one having the least financial impact on the survivors makes the most economic sense. The second part, about divorce, I would answer unequivocally no! Our marriage vows pledge love through sickness as well as health, until death parts us! (I believe death needs to be validated by burial.)

THEOLOGIAN:
It would depend on the circumstances. I'm thinking of a case where a Christian man did divorce a wife who was hopelessly ill with MS. Officially they are divorced, therefore the state is carrying all the expense so that the

husband and children will not be put into virtual bankruptcy by the expense of the mother's care in the facility.

Suppose there were no such recourse and my wife is in a position requiring medical expense that will leave me without any resources. My inclination would be to spend all the resources and take care of her in keeping with the promise "for better or worse until death do us part" and then trust God to provide for me. If children are involved and they would be left destitute, it becomes more complicated because I must provide for my own (1 Timothy 5:8) and I am, therefore, torn two ways. I think again I would opt for doing all I could with the resources at my command and depend on God to care for future needs — not in blind faith, but in confidence.

PASTOR C:

This is tougher than the first question. I'm not sure I can answer it. In anticipation of such a potential situation, however, it is possible for any of us to give a "Durable Power of Attorney" to our spouse, or some other person, so that in circumstances you cited or other "irreversible" situations no life-sustaining or prolonged treatments would be used. In a real sense, without such a legal document in hand, there is not much to do without an insurance policy that takes care of catastrophic illnesses.

PASTOR D:

I would urge them to get as accurate information as possible on: (1) alternate means of financing for the spouse's care; (2) medical prognosis of the spouse's condition; and (3) options that have not been considered. Regarding the long-term future of the surviving spouse, some projections should be discussed and considered. But I would *never* tell someone flat out that he or she should get a divorce.

PRIEST:

I would not want anyone to fall prey to the either/or choice between remaining married and suffering the financial drain or to abandon the patient through divorce in order to enjoy financial viability. Creative alternatives need to be explored with appropriate social services and funding agencies. Also, support services within the hospital, community and church need to be used.

None of those questioned believed in divorce; however, in talking to doctors, I found that many of their patients have been forced into that position. They are legally divorced, and as a result the terminally ill spouse is getting the necessary care. However, the couple still feel married and the patient is visited daily. It would be a tough situation to have to face.

But where does one draw the line? To again quote Judie Brown, president of the American Life League:

> There are powerful forces in our society—who are hard at work to redefine basic human needs as "treatment," the "expense" of which will have to be justified by the social usefulness of the patient. The person who is nearing death is obviously not contributing to society, we are told. He or she is just a burden, consuming time and money.
>
> Thus saith the American Medical Association, for one. Don't scoff! Doctors have become powermad before. In Germany, several years before the big death camps were built, the psychiatric and incurable hospitals were literally emptied out, saving a fortune in taxes for the Third Reich's many other vital projects.[5]

Some of the most difficult problems in the health care arena in our own nation were compounded when Medicare altered its payment program in 1984. Under the new system hospitals receive a specific amount according to the particular diagnosis of each patient. This does not take into consideration that patients with the same medical problem may require differing amounts of care and medication. Hospitals often are forced to release patients before those patients are physically ready to be moved to another facility or to go back to independent living.

Programs that provided various health services in senior centers have been eliminated or cut back. The person with a fixed income, one who exists on Social Security and perhaps a small pension, is soon bankrupted by hospital stays and unnecessary tests. Even if a person has a comfortable income, those expenses will wipe out his savings and put him in debt. It is frightening to discover how many travel this road to poverty and it is no wonder that senior suicides are on the rise.

The report of the President's Commission for the study of Ethical Problems in Medicine[6] referred to in chapter 10 also speaks of the financial problems caused by life-sustaining treatment: "The total expense of maintaining a patient who would not survive without the therapy can be substantial."

It goes on to say that decisions are sometimes made about the use of life-sustaining care with no regard to the high cost of the services and with little or no concern for the chance of survival. These decisions do not always reflect societal values. Not every method needs to be used for every patient. "Therapy must offer benefits proportionate to the costs — financial and otherwise."

The report does not state that society wants cost to be given priority in decisions on life-sustaining care, but that the cost must be considered.

It does explain that some small tests and minor treatment expenditures are out of proportion to the overall picture. "Over one-third of the 75 million chest X rays done in 1980 (at a cost of nearly $2 billion) were unnecessary." It also estimates that cardiac pacemakers have been used in many cases when they are not necessary — at a cost of about $280 million annually. Of the respiratory treatments ordered, 25 percent are deemed unnecessary. "Even when treatment is life-sustaining, in many cases patients and physicians agree that the patient's prognosis makes the treatment of so little benefit that it is not worth pursuing."

The Commission states, however: "Nor should discussions of cost-containment begin with consideration of life-sustaining treatments." The report recommends that the public be educated and that society develop rules for equal and acceptable limits in utilizing health care. For example, the decision to use CPR when cardiac arrest occurs has to be immediate as a delay means the patient is less likely to be revived. Many families of terminally ill patients order a "No Code" or "DNR" ("Do not resuscitate") placed on a patient's chart, which tells the staff there is to be no CPR.

The Commission states further:

> Resuscitation decisions are currently made with little regard to the costs incurred or to the manner in which costs are distributed.
>
> The Commission heard from a number of people, however, who wondered if providers and others should consider whether the costs of resuscitation are warranted for those patients for whom survival is unlikely and who would, in any case, suffer overwhelming disabilities and diseases.

To look at the subject from a doctor's point of view, a recent issue of the *Orange County Register* published an article by Dr. Peter Gott. Gott told a true story, illustrating what could happen to any doctor, anywhere.

The patient was an active octogenarian in fine health except for an occasional asthma attack. He called the doctor because he had had a night of difficult breathing. The doctor met him in the emergency room and the patient was given a machine treatment. When his breathing eased, the doctor suggested hospitalization for further treatment. The patient refused the offer, was given a prescription and left.

Later the same day he called back with more breathing problems. This time he was admitted. The following morning he "clearly needed another twenty-four hours of observation and treatment."

Since this was in 1986, after the Medicare changes, there were new requirements to be met. One was that before admitting the patient to the hospital the doctor must "notify a government agency known as a peer review organization." The conversation went something like this:

"Hello, this is Dr. Gott. I admitted a patient yesterday and would like a certification number, please."

"Yes. How do you spell it?"

"What?"

"Your name."

"Oh. *G-O-T-T.*"

"What's the patient's name?"

I gave it.

"Medicare number?"

I gave it.

"Date of birth?"

I gave it.

"Diagnosis?"

"Acute bronchial asthma."

"Why does he have to be in the hospital?"

"Because he can't breathe. He needed treatment."

"Did you do blood gases?"

"Not reported yet."

"Is he getting intravenous therapy?"

"No. So far he hasn't needed it."

"Well, what are you doing?"

"Giving oral bronchodilators, aerosolized treatment by nebulizer and cortisone."

"He can do that as an outpatient. I don't see that he needs hospitalization."

"He can't function at home. He's 80 and lives alone. He requires inhalation therapy."

"I still don't think he needs to be in the hospital."

"Well, I'm sorry you feel that way. We tried outpatient therapy and it didn't hold him at home. Are you going to refuse him?"

"I guess not . . . I don't know . . . all right, here is your number."

"Thank you. Goodbye."

Dr. Gott went on to say that he will be prepared for the

"game" the next time around. He also pointed out that although hospital costs have escalated, he questions if it is in patients' best interests to have such hospitalizations accepted or rejected by a faceless voice.[7]

Home care followed by a hospice program (when the patient is terminal) seems to be one way to avoid bankrupting a family with hospital costs. Although not every family is equipped to try at-home or home hospice care, it may be the only way from a financial standpoint.

A friend commented after reading this manuscript, "But you haven't given any definite answers to these questions."

My reply: "Of course not. God is the only one who knows the absolutes. There is nothing conclusive that will fit every situation. All we as mortals can do is study the facts, approach our decision with prayer, then decide what is best for our own individual situation. We must look to Scripture. The Bible is filled with comfort and can direct us to the right answers."

12 The Greatest Comfort

> *Don't be afraid of those who can kill only your bodies — but can't touch your soul! Fear only God who can destroy both soul and body in hell* (Matthew 10:28, TLB).
> *Salvation is found in no one else;*
> *for there is no other name under heaven given to men by which we must be saved* (Acts 4:12, NIV).

A SOUTHERN CALIFORNIA pastor had gone to a member's home to visit the small son who was sick. While there, he met the father's aunt who was having trouble with her throat and could hardly talk.

Some weeks later the aunt, now unable to talk at all, remembered the comfort the pastor had brought to the little boy, and she called her nephew and asked if he would bring the pastor to see her. They drove to her home in Azusa, and, after mutual greetings, she invited him into the library to "talk." She would have to communicate by writing. She told the pastor that she had cancer of the throat and would not live much longer. But she wasn't ready to die — what could she do?

The pastor explained that Jesus loved her, and that He had given His life so she could have forgiveness of sins and eternal life with the Father in heaven.

"You need to accept Him as your Savior, and put your life into His hands. Would you like to do that?"

Overcome with emotion, she began crying and could not answer the pastor.

He asked her again, "Would you like to invite Christ into your life?"

Trembling, she picked up her pen and wrote, *Yes*.

The pastor took both her hands and they prayed — he aloud, and she silently.

When they finished he asked her if she had accepted Christ. She answered yes, and began crying again, but this time it was a happy crying.

She wrote, *Will He give my voice back to me?*

The pastor answered, "Maybe not in this life, but the moment you enter into His presence you will be able to speak to anyone you want to."

Realizing the blessings to come, she cried again. Within six weeks she entered the Lord's presence.

Death a Celebration

Death should not be shrouded in black mourning clothes. If those who leave us belong to the Lord, they will go on to a glorious life where they will no longer suffer pain or discomfort.

This book is not only about death, but also about eternal life. Those who believe in God and have a personal relationship with His Son, Jesus Christ, know that when their final breath has left them and their heart is at rest, their life has just begun. God has provided a future paradise for them. Jesus said, "In my Father's house are many mansions: if it were not so, I would have told you. I go to prepare a place for you" (John 4:2, KJV).

Thus the most important thing for the one facing death is to be certain he has made peace with his Lord. Then death becomes a celebration — paradise awaits!

What a promise! But what about the person who is terminal and not sure of his salvation?

Our desire is to make the last days of a terminally ill

patient as comfortable and filled with hope as possible. What greater hope could we bring a dying person than to lead him or her to the assurance of an eternity in God's presence? What comfort could compare with a patient personally experiencing God's love within his illness?

However, people often are reluctant to talk to a dying person about death. The subject is an uncomfortable one — no one *likes* to talk about it, and we often go to extremes to avoid it. We don't want to remind the person of what's happening or to inflict pain. But we need to realize that we will not be *reminding* the person of his condition — it's already on his mind day and night.

Another possible reason for our reluctance to discuss death is mentioned by author and college instructor Dale V. Hardt in *Death: The Final Frontier:*

> Because Americans try to prolong life at almost any cost, it can be deduced that most Americans fear death. Hence, among other coping mechanisms, repression of death thoughts is apparent.[1]

Talking to the Patient

So how do you talk to someone who is dying? How do you bring up the subject of their death? Most likely, the questions you're thinking to yourself are just the thoughts you *should* voice, however hard they may be. Your friend knows that *you* know he is dying, and talking about it openly will help dispel some of the mystery and fear. It also reassures him that you care. Some questions you can ask to let that person know that you do care are:

- How do you feel?
- What does the doctor say?
- How is your family handling this?

I spoke with pastors, priests, chaplains and lay people about ministering to the dying. Their responses showed a wide variety of experiences and approaches. One chaplain said, "If the person can admit that he is dying, we have a base line on which we can start. We discuss where he wants to die — at home or in the hospital — and how he feels about dying. This opens the door to discover if he fears, accepts or welcomes death." When we know more about how the person feels, we know more about how to approach him.

Incidentally, don't say, "I know how you feel" just so you can identify with him and feel less uncomfortable yourself. This is inappropriate unless you *have* been in the same situation and you *do* know how it feels. Recognize that your discomfort comes from being painfully aware that *I'm alive and he's dying.*

One hospital volunteer in Loma Linda, California, has found that terminal patients will open up when they know that she sincerely wants to know how they're feeling. Because Mary Jean Jennings was herself healed of cancer, she can easily establish rapport with others who are facing death. But she assures us that we don't have to have that common understanding to show that we're concerned.

"Basically, ask them how they feel, and listen," says Jennings. "While they're talking, be praying. Sympathize with them. Let them know that you care and want to help if there's any way you can. It takes time. You can't just rush in, wanting to score a point."

Talking about the subject is the place to start, but you must realize that your part in providing comfort doesn't stop at getting death out into the open. You need then to point your dying loved one toward life.

Witnessing to the Dying

It seems we become particularly intimidated when we think about talking to a dying person about his relationship with the Lord. In fact, we have a tendency to expect the hospital chaplain to take care of this need, or we tend to leave it to the preacher. We need to recognize two things about this approach: (1) Hospital chaplains usually are not allowed to initiate any talk about a person's salvation (which could be perceived as denominationalism); and (2) the privilege and responsibility of introducing a person to Jesus Christ is not limited to the preachers and pastors of our churches.

Bill Bright says in *Witnessing Without Fear:* "Loving others, showing them Jesus Christ in word and deed, is not a job for pastors or ministry workers only. It's a joyous task to which God has commissioned everyone who calls himself a Christian."[2] It is for us, the friends and families who are the most concerned about the patients, to reach out to them in love and try to meet their deepest needs.

The experiences I have had, and the people I have talked with, draw me to the conclusion that it's safe to assume a dying person wants to talk. He is really concerned about spiritual things. More than one counselor has said, "Terminally ill patients are easier to talk to about their souls than anyone else."

Even knowing that, the subject of death may still be uncomfortable to you. If it is, though, imagine how much scarier it must seem to someone who doesn't know the Lord, someone who has no assurance as to what's in store for him beyond the grave. How can you help him or her face that future with acceptance and peace?

Some of the questions you can ask to start spiritual conversations are:

- Have you thought much about what happens after you die?
- Are you afraid of dying?
- Are you interested in spiritual things?
- Have you ever thought about becoming a Christian?
- What do you think about heaven, and about eternal life after death?
- Do you fear leaving anyone behind?
- Do you think they would be comforted to know where you will be for eternity?
- Have you come to faith in the Lord Jesus?
- God has helped me in my troubles, although they're not the same as yours. Do you know Him?
- How do you feel about Him?
- How would you like to *know* — beyond a doubt — that you'll go to heaven when you die?

"My big question is," I asked one spiritual leader, "what do you say to an agnostic about death — the one who has never tried to get close to the Lord or says he doesn't even want to hear about God?"

"I counter that kind of a statement with, 'OK, we won't talk about God. Let's talk about you instead.' "

I could see very quickly how some of the same questions listed above could be used to lead even that person into a spiritual conversation.

This same leader said, "We need to remember that people today really are searching for an intimate relationship with God." But as the Ethiopian eunuch asked Stephen in Acts, chapter 8: How can they know where to find what they seek unless someone guides them?

Leading the Way

When one pastor from Southern California was preparing to fly to the Philippine Islands to hold some meetings for a native pastor, a friend asked him to go to the hospital in Manila and call on her niece who was dying with cancer.

The host pastor picked him up at the airport and they drove directly to the hospital. They entered the patient's room, and the visiting pastor explained who he was and why he was there.

"I understand you have a terminal illness," he said gently. "Are you ready to face that? How do you feel about it?"

"I can handle the sickness," she replied, "but I don't want to die. I'm not ready for that."

"Are you a Christian?" he asked.

"I don't know."

While the host Philippine pastor silently prayed, the visiting pastor explained to the young woman what a Christian is and how a person can become a Christian through accepting the death, burial and resurrection of Christ as payment for sin. He also explained how she could face her illness and death with the power of Christ. Then he asked her if she would like to become a Christian.

Her answer was, "Yes, I would. I've always wanted to, but didn't know how."

They all three joined hands and prayed, the visiting pastor leading the patient in a prayer of invitation for Christ to come into her life and make her His own.

The two pastors saw a remarkable change come over the woman as she realized with joy that God loved her and that now she had a permanent home with Him in heaven. They were not aware of how it may have affected her physically, but they heard later that she went into remission and got strong enough to make the visit to Singapore that she had planned. She returned to the hospital in Manila for more medication, then came back to live in the Los Angeles area again, where she spent two more years with her family and friends, witnessing and sharing Christ with them, and enjoying life, before the Lord finally called her home.

How different the end of this woman's life would have been if she had not met Jesus. And how sad that she had to wait until so near the end of her life. Yet meet Him she did—because someone cared enough to go to her boldly with the gospel.

When you have a friend or loved one who is facing death, you must realize the urgency of the situation. This is no time to be timid.

Guiding Principles

It will be helpful to be aware of certain principles as you prepare to speak with a dying patient.

First, before you go to speak with him (or her), it is necessary to pray. A person who is terminally ill needs comfort far beyond what you can provide. Only the Lord knows his dreams, his fears, his joys and regrets. Pray that God will begin to work in his heart so that he will be prepared to open up and turn to Him.

Trust God for the right words. There is no way you could know what the person most needs to hear, but God *does* know, and He will give you the words—or tell you to remain silent. Don't be afraid of those times of silence. Your presence is more of a comfort than you could ever realize until you are in the same situation yourself. When you think about talking to your dying friend or family menber, realize that he doesn't expect you to know the perfect things to say. He just needs to know that you care.

We also need to be aware of the fact that people who are dying generally go through five stages of mourning. As recognized by Dr. Elisabeth Kubler-Ross, a leader in psychiatric theory regarding dying patients, those states are shock and denial, anger, bargaining, depression, and acceptance. The way your friend initially responds to you may be colored by which stage he's dealing with at the time. So be patient and understanding with him.

"Assuring them of God's love is very important," says Mary Jean Jennings, the Loma Linda hospital volunteer. "But that is not easy to do because a lot of people think that because they're ill, God doesn't love them. Our earthly life is only part of the whole, where God wants us to live with Him forever. The life we'll live after this is so far better than what we can imagine. That's probably the most encouraging thing we can say."

Think of your role as that of a comforter and guide, helping to make the patient's last days anxiety-free and guiding him to think about his eternal destiny. Many people spend years being distressed over a loved one's death because they were afraid to talk about spiritual things with him while he was living. This is your opportunity to sensitively search out your friend's spiritual position. What do you — and what does he — have to lose?

You must remember, though, that it is not your responsibility to change his heart — God does that. Witnessing isn't considered "successful" by how people respond. Rather, *successful witnessing* is simply taking the initiative to share Christ in the power of the Holy Spirit, and then *leaving the results to God*.

Remembering the openness of people's hearts to spiritual things during a severe illness will increase your courage to take the initiative. Payson Gregory, ordained minister and volunteer hospital chaplain, says, "You find that when people are hurting, they're open. You don't know what God's doing in them. He's dealing with hearts constantly here. Every day I pray, *Lord, lead me to the right people today.*"

Once you've asked some questions and steered the conversation onto spiritual ground, be sensitive. If the person is noticeably resistant to what you're saying, ask if you may leave something to read — a small tract.* Gregory says, "I use a lot of literature around the hospital. Every pocket in my coat is full. Some people aren't open to talk but will take literature. Often I'll leave it on the table and come back later and see them reading it."

Decision Time

If they *are* open to talking with you about spiritual things, sensitively present to them a simple outline of what it means to place their trust in Christ as their Savior. The evangelistic booklet "The Four Spiritual Laws" is an excellent, step-by-step presentation of man's need for forgiveness, God's offering of a Savior and His promise of eternal rest with Him in heaven. If someone is unfamiliar with the gospel message, reading through this booklet with him will make the issues clear and help bring the person to a point of confidently believing that he will be with God in heaven. Additional Scripture verses are listed in the back of the booklet for Christians who aren't sure of their place in heaven.

Finally, whether or not the person is ready right then to place his faith in Christ, offer to pray with him. "Even if he doesn't respond," said Gregory, "I will pray with him: 'Jesus, thanks for dying on the cross. Help _____ to know you and trust you.' "

If the person *does* want to come into a relationship with Christ, you can lead him in a prayer such as the following:

---

* To obtain gospel tracts and other helpful Christian literature, contact your local Christian bookstore or write: Good News Publishers, 9825 W. Roosevelt Rd., Westchester, IL 60153.

Lord Jesus, I need You. Thank You for dying on the cross for my sins. I open the door of my life and receive You as my Savior and Lord. Thank You for forgiving my sins and giving me eternal life. Take control of the throne of my life. Make me the kind of person You want me to be.

If you've never talked to anyone about eternal life in Christ, you might want to read *Witnessing Without Fear,* by Bill Bright, founder and president of the interdenominational ministry Campus Crusade for Christ. In this practical book Bright explains what helped him become a confident witness for Jesus Christ.

Don't be afraid to be bold in your sensitivity. You have the most important message in the world to offer, and your dying loved one has an eternity to gain.

*Five areas to explore when you
must make . . .*

13 | The
Final Decision

> *And when we obey him, every path he guides us on is
> fragrant with his lovingkindness and his truth*
> (Psalm 25:10, TLB).

For variety in my quiet time this year, I decided to use
the *One Year Bible*. Leviticus 19:32 was part of a recent
reading: "Rise in the presence of the aged, show respect for
the elderly and revere your God. I am the LORD" (NIV). In
drawing this book to a close, I'm certain God led me to that
verse. Certain, because it contains a "key" to the dilemma
of the aged and dying. It is interesting and pertinent that
God combined respect for the elderly and reverence for Him
in the same sentence. We must, especially if we wear the
name "Christian" and claim reverence for the Lord, follow
the admonition to respect the elderly and revere God.

This book has not been developed as an absolute directive in the matter of life support and care of the elderly and
infirmed. Rather, it is a compilation of factual information
and true human experiences which have been gathered
prayerfully to become a road map of the various routes
family members may travel to ensure a more comfortable
dying process for their loved ones and a sense of peace for
themselves.

For some, a portion of that peace is found when a loved one is released to our heavenly Father. Madeline L'Engle draws the story of her mother to a close by explaining that she was in New York when she felt something—a feeling that she must call home to check on her mother. Her son told her, "Grandmother died about four this afternoon."

Later, when asked how she was feeling, L'Engle replied, "All I feel is gratitude and joy. I'm going to grieve, and I'm going to cry eventually, but it will be right and proper grief."[1]

In the final chapter she expresses her feelings in a delightful manner: "The pattern has shifted; we have changed places in a dance. I am no longer anybody's child. I have become the grandmother."[2] A beautiful tribute to a close and warm relationship between a mother and daughter, a relationship that was not marred by the trauma of the mother's care nor by her death.

For Christians, death can be beautiful. L'Engle's story took me back to the night my father died, just a few months before my mother had her first stroke.

He had been hospitalized, and because of the hour, the lights were low and the corridors quiet as the nurse and I silently walked toward his room. I dreaded entering that room—I had seen friends and relatives in their caskets, but never anyone dead in a hospital bed, especially not someone I dearly loved.

But my apprehension vanished as we entered. The presence of the Lord completely filled the room. There was a peace both in the room and on Dad's face, a peace that had not been present through the long time of his suffering. I knew my father was with Jesus and I wanted to shout "Hallelujah!" and waken all the sleeping patients, and tell them that my dad had finally found eternal, sought-after peace and was with Jesus. Only his body lay in that bed. Dad was in heaven!

I, too, eventually cried, but it was a happy kind of grief, a peaceful grief.

I have always been able to find peace and solace in my

Bible and in other writings. Through my writing and speaking years, I have discovered many literary gems. My files bulge with them. In a pamphlet with a six-cent price and no author to credit for the interesting thoughts, I found the following philosophy: "What comes after death? Playing with that question can be sort of a parlor game." The author suggests that one can ignore the question "for fear of commercializing goodness by tying it to rewards and punishments."

Then the author points out how practical the question is, though strangely so. It suggests that when man loses the biblical idea of a life after death, he tends to play a fast game with life. History has proven that cultures who lose their belief in immortality tend toward "tyranny and social evils — because temporary creatures get less respect than immortal souls."

The author further explains that even the Bible "cannot give us guidebook descriptions of the next world because our imaginings are limited to the sort of things we have seen." Some people get tied up in the idea of reincarnation, and they "believe in dreary rounds of rebirths in other bodies," but we Christians have a faith that directs us to "endless vistas of beauty and glory and joy." As children of God, we know His love through His Son Jesus, and that love is one "on which we can always depend."[3]

A strong faith can surmount the apprehensions that face us when life-support decisions must be made. Medical technology has moved faster than our ability to think through the problems which have and will continue to arise.

People used to get sick, then sicker. The doctor came to the house to see the terminal patient. The next stage was difficulty in eating so the food was pureed. Then the move was to a liquid diet. Eventually, the patient died, right in his home.

Then we invented hospitals and the sick were taken there and much the same pattern was followed. Next came the marvelous discovery called cardiopulmonary resuscitation. This gave the staff the ability to start a heart that had stopped. We then taught everyone in the hospital to do this and it became a routine order that *anyone* whose heart stopped was to be given CPR. As a result, one no longer goes to a hospital to die.

To quote an ICU nurse, "We won't allow people to die in hospitals!" And this is partly why we as individuals have to make these life-or-death decisions. Hospitals are equipped to keep patients alive. I certainly don't suggest that hospitals go into the killing business, but sometimes I wonder if medical science hasn't outsmarted itself. We no longer allow death to enter even the terminally ill person's life if there is any possible way to delay it.

We have put a value on life, and a value on death, and the ability to extend life has caused us to have to think about how we balance those values. Now we must clarify them. Whose values are they? And what priorities do they hold? We must approach the necessary decisions through an effective, ethical decision-making process.

In the prologue of *To Live and to Die: When, Why and How* Robert H. Williams describes the issue:

> There are times when the merits of dying outweigh those of living. The prime purpose for living is to engage in mentation, the act of thinking. A person who will never have mentation usually serves no desirable purpose in life, but he will experience no suffering. Pleasant mentation stimulates desire for living. Mentation associated with marked and persistent suffering prompts desire for death.[4]

An example of suffering that prompted a desire for death is found in the story of a 67-year-old man who suffered a stroke of such force that he was totally paralyzed except for facial expressions. He was in what the medical profession calls a "locked in" syndrome, being kept alive by machines. His only means of communication was the ability to mouth words and use the expression in his eyes. He contracted pneumonia and because he was on a ventilator he was in extreme discomfort.

After being in ICU for four weeks he mouthed the words, "Please take this thing [meaning the ventilator] away!" He was fully aware that without the ventilator his respiratory system could not function.

His supportive family was shocked by his request. Although they knew there was no chance for his recovery, they did not want to face the thought of losing their husband and father. He could have recovered from the pneumonia but the paralysis would have remained.

The ventilator was uncomfortable and the process of suctioning out the secretions was miserable. Eventually the patient might have been able to be taken to his home but the ventilator would have had to go with him. Despite his inability to verbalize aloud, there was no doubt about his desire to die.

If the family had not called the paramedics when he became ill, he would have died at home. But as anyone who has faced a like situation asks, How can you sit and wait, and watch for death, when there might be hope of life through medical intervention?

This man's family met with the hospital's bioethic committee and asked questions such as: *Can you eliminate his pain?* The answer was negative because of his neurological condition. *Is the suctioning process painful?* The answer was affirmative. *What will his death be like if the ventilator is removed?* They feared a suffocating death would be horrible. The committee explained that medication could be given to assure there would be no discomfort during the dying process.

Next the family discussed the situation with the patient. It was clear to them what he wanted. The doctor spoke to him and explained what they would do to keep him comfortable through the process if he still wanted to die. The patient asked for time alone, then met again with his family. His decision was to be medicated and taken off the ventilator. Within three hours he died peacefully, his loved ones at his side.

The Decision-making Process

In order to help a family reach a decision when it becomes necessary, a bioethic committee, a clergyman and the hospital chaplain should be part of the consulting team. If the hospital does not have a bioethics committee, the family should meet with a pastor or hospital chaplain, the doctor, a lawyer and a non-involved person to assemble and discuss the facts. Listed are the areas that should be considered and the questions that must be answered.

1. *Medical Condition*
   a. What is the prognosis and survival rate?
   b. How much risk will there be?
   c. What treatments are involved?
   d. What is the success rate of the treatment?
   e. How certain is it that the treatment will work?
   f. How much pain can be expected?
   g. Will the benefits outweigh discomforts of the procedure?

2. *Social and Religious Implications*
   a. What is the patient's family situation (single, married, etc.)?
   b. What will be the effect on his immediate family members?
   c. Is there a church that will be supportive?
   d. Is the patient spiritually ready to face death?

3. *Caregivers and/or Family Members*
   a. What are their opinions?
   b. Is there conflict within the family, or are their views in agreement with each other?
   c. Are their views in agreement with the patient?
   d. What are their options?

4. *Legal Aspects*
   a. What are the patient's wishes regarding life support?
   b. Has the patient signed a legal document regarding his wishes?
   c. Is the patient competent and willing to state his wishes in such a document?
   d. What is the hospital's policy on heroic measures?

5. *The Expense Factor*
   a. What are the estimated costs involved?
   b. Will the benefits outweigh the expected expense incurred?
   c. What financial support options does the family have?
   d. What outside resources might be available?

Finding the Peace

It is important to realize that when a decision must be made, one may *never* feel certain about rightness of that decision. If time has been spent in prayer and in the Bible, though, you can have a strong feeling that the answer—whatever it is—has come from the Lord.

When we faced the decision about my mother, I took time to pray—while my sister waited on the other end of the phone line and wondered if I had heard her. I had to hesitate, to wait until I felt the "peace that passeth all understanding." I had to have time to experience the assurance that all was right. With it came a relaxing of my tenseness and I knew the decision was the correct one.

In *Concerning Them That Are Asleep,* Daniel Hoffman Martin says, "Death is a part of the cycle of change which God has established for everyone He has created."[5]

Facing death is not easy. In *When All You've Ever Wanted Isn't Enough,* Rabbi Harold S. Kushner tells of a discussion he had with a friend, a clergyman he admired. They talked about ministering to the dying. The friend told of a parishioner who had been hospitalized with an inoperable brain tumor and how the friend simply could not bring himself to visit the patient.

Kushner explained, "I would guess that you are afraid of dying—it's nothing to be ashamed of; lots of people are—and that is why seeing someone your own age dying is so hard for you to deal with."

He goes on to tell the friend that he (Kushner) was not afraid to die but that he was not yet ready to die, either. He explained that it is often not a fear of death but the fear of "never having lived, that we never figured out what life was for," that frightens us.[6]

Is it a fear of death that makes some people want to keep a loved one alive far beyond the point of his possible recovery? Death is not to be feared. Jesus died that we might have eternal life.

An expert in the bioethic field, a man who meets with families facing these decisions, talked about biblical ethics to a church group—and cautioned that we are *not* to take human life. To kill is not the way out of this dilemma, he said. And no person should be considered useless, or too old, or sociopathic, or whatever one might deem to be of no value. None of these conditions gives cause to take a human life. However, there is nothing in biblical ethics that states life is to be prolonged with unusual or heroic measures. In fact, we have been warned in the Bible about the danger of idolizing the body by trying to maintain life at any cost. Jesus said, "He who finds his life will lose it, and he who loses his life for my sake will find it" (Matthew 10:39, RSV).

The only answer to the question, Should we allow Mother to die? is to be as informed as possible on all the issues surrounding the subject and to know all the facts of the individual case, to walk closely with the Lord, and to put your trust in Him. Through prayer and an in-depth look at the Scriptures, seek God's answers for your special situation. The Holy Spirit, the Comforter, has been promised to us, and He is available for help. Be patient while waiting on Him to fill you with His peace.

One Scripture that has helped me in many times of trial is Romans 5:3-5 (TLB):

We can rejoice, too, when we run into problems and trials for we know that they are good for us—they help us learn to be patient. And patience develops strength of character in us and helps us trust God more each time we use it until finally our hope and faith are strong and steady. Then, when that happens, we are able to hold our heads high no matter what happens and know that all is well, for we know how dearly God loves us, and we feel this warm love everywhere within us because God has given us the Holy Spirit to fill our hearts with his love.

 # Epilogue

IN THE RESEARCH I've done for this book, the most compassionate and truthful item I've read is the following, written by Chuck Bowden for *USA Today*.

WATCHING DEATH BECOME A REALITY

Early that morning, we had the switches tripped and watched her spin off into eternity. The heart was finished, the body weary after 70-some years.

The doctors had rolled her into surgery three days before, opened her up, and shut her back up. There was nothing to be done, they said.

Letting someone die is an act that divides people on ethical and political grounds. We can keep people breathing who are seemingly dead because we have built machines to do just that. Before that morning, I had read articles on the matter. This time I did not have to read about it.

I had come off the mountain after two days in the snow, and when I got home my wife called and said it was her mother. For the next three days, I lived in the intensive care unit. We made periodic visits to her room, listened to a machine go "whoosh" while working her lungs, and watched her heartbeat skip across a screen.

My wife wept at times and held her mother. She would talk to her and tell her she was brave and good. There was no response, but that did not mean the message was not received. There are some things that the mind cannot prove, but the heart cannot doubt.

I would take breaks and walk outside; spring was in the air and the trees were in leaf, the birds singing with lust and hope. I could taste life. And then I would go back into the room, see arms full of needles, the tubes streaming into the nostrils, hear the sounds, and watch the screen where the heart danced out its last patterns.

Finally the doctors said there was no hope for recovery. We decided to turn off the machines, and we sat there as she slowly died. The pulse wandered downward, and the line on the screen gradually flattened. My wife held her mother and talked soothingly. And then she was dead.

I have nothing to tell people who want a quick ethical fix for these matters, a kind of penicillin for their souls. I have no more interest in the articles debating the issues.

I will tell you where this matter of life and death belongs and where it should stay: in the room I was in, where an old woman trapped in a finished body, died in the arms of the daughter who loved her.

Appendix A

Organizations That May Help
(Some of these have not been investigated)

American Association of Homes for the Aged
1129 20th St. NW, Suite 400
Washington, DC 20036
(Write for information)

American Life League
P.O. Box 1350
Garrisonville, VA 20436
(703) 659-4171
(Pro-life service organization)

American Society on Aging
833 Market St., Suite 516
San Francisco, CA 94103
(415) 543-2617
(Training center on aging; information center on resources)

Americans United for Life (Right-to-Life)
343 S. Dearborn, Suite 1804
Chicago, IL 60604
(312) 786-9494
(Concerned with protection of human life at all stages of development)

Alzheimer's Disease & Related Disorders Association
70 E. Lake
Chicago, IL 60601
(800) 621-0379; in Illinois (800) 572-6037
(More than 160 chapters and 1000 support groups nationwide)

Association for Death Education & Counseling
2211 Arthur Ave.
Lakewood, OH 44107
(216) 228-0334
(Upgrade quality of death education and patient care in hospitals, care facilities, etc.)

Beverly Foundation
841 S. Fair Oaks
Pasadena, CA 91105
(818) 792-2292
(Encourage "creative aging" programs for long-term care service systems)

California Medical Association
P.O. Box 7690
San Francisco, CA 94103-7690
(Durable Power of Attorney for Health Care forms and other information)

Catholic Health Association of the United States
4455 Woodson Road
St. Louis, MO 63134
(Christian Affirmation of Life brochure and other information)

Children of Aging Parents
2761 Trenton Rd.
Levittown, PA 19056
(Will refer you to nearby local support groups or help you start one)

Christian Action Council
701 W. Broad St., Suite 405
Falls Church, VA 22046
(Euthanasia education packet)

Church of Brethren Homes & Hospital Association
1451 Dundee
Elgin, IL 60120
(312) 742-5100
(Shares common concerns and programs of service to hospitalized or aging people)

Concern for Dying
250 W. 57th St.
New York, NY 10107
(212) 246-6962
(Prevention of futile prolongation of the dying process)

Ebenezer Society
2500 Park Ave.
Minneapolis, MN 55404
(612) 879-1467
(Offers nusing home care, provides home services to help persons remain in their own home as long as possible)

Elder Abuse Registry
(Orange County Medical Assoc. Auxiliary)
300 S. Flower St.
Orange, CA 92668
(714) 834-4668
(Supportive services)

Episcopal Society for Ministry on Aging
R.D. 4, Box 146A
Milford, NJ 08848
(201) 995-2885
(Serves spiritual, mental and physical needs of older persons and families)

Euthanasia Educational Council
250 West 57th Street
New York, NY 10019
(Living Will/Directive for Health Care forms and other information)

Fletcher Hills Presbyterian Church
455 Church Way
El Cajon, CA 92020
(Respite Caregivers Program setup and training information)

Hemlock Society
P.O. Box 66218
Los Angeles, CA 90066
(213) 391-1871
(Self-deliverance for the dying)

Hospital Christian Fellowship
P.O. Box 4004
San Clemente, CA 92672
(714) 496-7655
(Taking our Lord's commission in Mark 16:15 as applying to hospital and health services)

Hospice Education Institute
P.O. Box 713
Five Essex Sq., Suite 3-B
Essex, CT 06426
(203) 767-1620
(Maintains speakers. Bureau developing data base of hospice and hospice-type programs, (800) 331-1620)

Human Life Alliance of Minnesota, Inc.
P.O. Box 293
Minneapolis, MN 55440
(612) 925-9888
(A national pro-life organization)

Human Life Center
International Anti-Euthanasia Task Force
University of Steubenville
Steubenville, OH 43952
(614) 282-9953   (612) 542-3120

Jewish Association for Service for the Aged
40 W. 68th St.
New York, NY 10023
(Provides services necessary to enable older adults to remain in their
community)

Legal Counsel for the Elderly
1909 K St. NW
Washington, DC 20049
(202) 662-4933
(Direct free legal services to DC residents age 60 plus)

Legal Services for the Elderly
132 W. 43rd St., 3rd Floor
New York, NY 10036
(212) 459-1340
(Advise and litigate problems of the elderly)

National Association for Home Care
519 C St. NE
Stanton Park
Washington, DC 20002
(Clearinghouse regarding home-care agencies)

National Association of Area Agencies on Aging
600 Maryland Ave. SW, Suite 208
Washington, DC 20024
     National Association of State Units (same address for referrals to ser-
vices in other states)
     National Institute on Adult Daycare (same street address but W Wing
100 for information to enhance daycare programs)

National Council on the Aging, Inc.
P.O. Box 7227
Ben Franklin Station
Washington, DC 20044
(National directory of caregiver support groups)

National Hospice Organization
1901 North Myer Dr., Suite 902
Arlington, Virgina 22209
(At least one organization in every state. Write for information. Peer group networking)

National Rehabilitation Information Center
(800) 34NARIC or (202) 635-5826
(Provides information on products and resources needed for the caregivers aid)

RSVP (Retired Senior Volunteer Program)

Region I: 441 Stuart St., 9th floor
Boston, MA 02116
(617) 223-4501

Region II: Jacob V. Javits Federal Bldg.
26 Federal Plaza, Suite 16121
New York, NY 10278
(212) 264-4747

Region III: U.S. Customs House
2nd & Chestnut Sts., Rm. 108
Philadelphia, PA 19106
(215) 587-9972

Region IV: 101 Marietta St. NW, Suite 1003
Atlanta, GA 30323
(404) 221-2859

Region V: 10 West Jackson Blvd., 3rd Floor
Chicago, IL 60604
(312) 353-5107

Region VI:1100 Commerce, Rm 6B11
Dallas, TX 75242
(214) 353-5107

Region VIII: Executive Tower Bldg., Suite 2930
1405 Curtis St.
Denver, CO 80202
(303) 844-2671

Region IX: 211 Main St., Rm. 530
San Francisco, CA 94105
(415) 974-0673

Region X: 1111 Third Ave., Suite 330
Seattle, WA 98101
(206) 442-1558

(These are main area offices which can direct you to the nearest group. They believe seniors are the answer, not the problem, and can be active in all areas of community service including aid to the aged and disabled.)

Senior Services for South Sound
222 N. Columbia
Olympia, WA 98501
(206) 943-6188
(Information and assistance/case management services)

Society for the Right to Die
250 W. 57th
New York, NY 10107
(212) 246-6973
(In support of dying with dignity, directive forms and other information)

These are suggested places to gain information and/or assistance in organizations with diverse goals. Check, too, with your local hospitals. Many have hospice programs as well as support groups, caregivers and/or programs for caregivers.

Appendix B

Group Studies And Discussions

I. This Discussion Guide was developed by California Health Decisions of Orange, California, to determine the opinions of a variety of individuals on the subject of life support.

To use in a discussion group, I would suggest that copies be passed out for each person to ponder and complete. Then divide the main group into small groups of no more than 6 to 8 and discuss each situation. Next, return to the larger group, and complete the study by exploring the group's opinion.

CALIFORNIA HEALTH DECISIONS
Discussion Guide
Directions:

The following statements refer to various ethical issues in health care. Please consider each statement and indicate whether your response *is closer to* agree, disagree, or not sure. Most of the statements need further clarification, which will take place during the group discussion.

1. If I am in a situation where I am not able to speak for myself and a decision has to made about using technology to prolong my life, I am confident that an appropriate decision will be made on my behalf.

      agree ( ) disagree ( ) not sure ( )

2. If my close relative is in a coma and not expected to recover, I should have the right to direct the doctors to withhold artificial feeding.

      agree ( ) disagree ( ) not sure ( )

3. The right of patients to refuse life-prolonging medical treatment should take precedence over other factors, such as doctors' fear of liability, family disagreements, etc.

      agree ( ) disagree ( ) not sure ( )

4. The government should be involved in deciding whether newborns with serious disabilities should be treated or not, rather than leave those decisions to the parents.

agree ( ) disagree ( ) not sure ( )

5. The quality of health services for long-term care patients is as good as can be expected.

    agree ( ) disagree ( ) not sure ( )

6. Everyone in the United States should have adequate health care regardless of ability to pay.

    agree ( ) disagree ( ) not sure ( )

7. We should make sure that the basic health care needs of all people are met before spending more money on the development of high-technology medicine.

    agree ( ) disagree ( ) not sure ( )

8. There should be a "means test" for Medicare patients, whereby patients over 65 who can afford it would pay more for their own medical care and receive less from the government.

    agree ( ) disagree ( ) not sure ( )

9. All pregnant women should have access to prenatal care.

    agree ( ) disagree ( ) not sure ( )

10. We would be better off if we had a national health care plan whereby health care would be provided by a government agency to anyone who wanted it, at little or no cost.

    agree ( ) disagree ( ) not sure ( )

11. If it would reduce the cost of health care, we should have a system whereby people are required to wait longer for nonemergency health services.

    agree ( ) disagree ( ) not sure ( )

12. California's health system should include economic incentives aimed at encouraging healthy life styles.

    agree ( ) disagree ( ) not sure ( )

13. Everyone who needs expensive life-saving procedures (such as organ transplants and open heart surgery) should have an equal chance at having them, regardless of ability to pay, age, social status, or other non-medical factors.

    agree ( ) disagree ( ) not sure ( )

14. Most of the issues listed above fall into six general categories. Please check *three* that are of most concern to you.

    ____assuring health care for everyone

    ____protecting patients' rights

    ____deciding about treatment for seriously ill newborns

    ____increasing quality of health care for the elderly and chronically ill _____deciding how health resources should be allocated

_____analyzing the appropriate use of high-technology medicine

Please list other issues of concern to you.

_____

_____

15. If you could make three recommendations for change in the current system of providing health care, what would they be?

1._____

2._____

3._____

II. Another group of questions was worked out by Gloria Davenport to be used as discussion starters:

SOME ISSUES/DILEMMAS TO BE CONSIDERED

1. Is medical science prolonging dying . . . or living?
2. Is society making the body sacred, forgetting the soul . . . thus demonstrating a fear of death?
3. Is the church willing to take a stand on assisted death?
4. Should society spend $1 billion a year to keep irreversibly comatose patients alive . . . often against their earlier expressed will (e.g., the Brophy case)?
5. Should artificial feeding (nasal or gastric tubes, etc.) be considered a medical intervention interfering with the right to die (e.g., the Brophy/Bouvia cases)?
6. Should 80% of Medicare funds be spent on the last two months of life, often against the patient's will?
7. Should millions be spent on extremely premature, *seriously* ill or malfunctioning babies when low income mothers are unable to obtain prenatal care (1300 in Orange County in 1986)?
8. Should transplants be available only to those who can afford them or who can reach the mass media?

Many different facets must be considered in the area of euthanasia and medical care. These points should be discussed and considered before they become matters of necessity!

III. Have the group divide into smaller groups and pretend they are a bioethic committee (remember that the family always meets with the committee to talk the problems out). The following fictitious situations represent what a bioethic group might have to face:

1. An 81-year-old patient had a severe stroke which caused paralysis on her right side and left her with difficulty in speaking. She has been in a nursing home because she is unable to care for her needs alone. Now the doctor has discovered cancer in her stomach and recommends surgery followed by chemotherapy and/or radiation treatments. Patient is of sound mind and wants no more medical treatment. Her children, however, do not all agree with their mother's wishes. Her husband died of cancer two years ago after a long illness. The mother will accept whatever the family and the committee agree to. What is your decision?

2. A 78-year-old male with leukemia has had extensive chemotherapy with the result that his blood is no longer able to make platelets. He has been hospitalized for almost two months and the treatment and constant testing has worn him out. He wants all testing and treatment stopped. He asks to be kept comfortable and allowed to die. Family members hate to watch him suffer, but don't know what to do. They have a date with the bioethic committee. What will you as a committee recommend?

3. A 39-year-old mother of two teenagers has Hodgkin's disease which has resulted in paralysis. She has been through months of chemotherapy and is presently in a semiconscious state. She has begged the doctors to prolong her life under any and all circumstances. They have complied, but it is most difficult for the husband and children to watch her suffer. It is also a terrible financial burden and threatens the funds they had saved for the children's college education. This family, too, has sought the help of the bioethic committee. What will be your suggestions for the family?

Appendix C

AARP (American Association of Retired Persons) has worked out this program on aging for church use:

How to Observe or Celebrate
A Sunday or Sabbath on Aging
IN YOUR CONGREGATION

Here's an idea to get your own congregation into ACTION. Designate a Sunday or Sabbath as a special occasion to celebrate the needs and potentialities of older persons within your congregation and the larger community and to symbolize a faith stance about aging which the religious community needs to share as the later years of life become a major agenda item for the entire society.

A special Sunday or Sabbath might include such elements as:

1. A special order of worship prepared by a committee including older members and using older persons in parts of the service.

2. Use of one or more of the Ten New Hymns on Aging and the Later Years. One copy is available free from the AARP Fulfillment Office, 1909 K St., N.W., Washington, D.C. 20049. For quantity needs write to the IRL office at the same address. The booklet contains texts of ten new hymns with metrical indices and tune suggestions.

3. Suggest a sermon or presentation on an appropriate topic such as "Accept Your Age," or "Overcoming Age Fright."

4. A discussion program in one or more adult classes on "The Role of Religion in the Later Years of Life," "Facing Loneliness," "The Aging Experience and the Life Process," "What the Bible Says About Aging and Older Persons," or other topics.

5. A fellowship meal for *all* members of the congregation. The program could feature: presentations by the presidents of the local Retired Teachers Association units or the chapters of the American Association of Retired Persons; a film such as THE THIRD AGE: THE NEW GENERATION; or contributions being made by older members both in the congregation and in the community.

6. Following the service of celebration or other event, the congregation might go to a nearby retirement facility or nursing home and share in a brief liturgy and/or reception for the residents.

7. A literature exhibit in the foyer or other location in the church or synagogue to include materials from the local library and AARP. Pastors, rabbis or other officials should inquire about free literature samples by writing the Interreligious Liaison Office, 1909 K St., N.W., Washington, D.C. 20049.

Notes

Chapter 2

1. *Euthanasia Educational Packet* (Falls Church, VA: Christian Action Council), p. 6.
2. Jerry B. Wilson, *Death by Decision* (Philadelphia: The Westminster Press, 1975), p. 28.
3. Jessamyn West, *The Woman Said Yes* (New York: Harcourt Brace Jovanovich, Inc., 1976), p. 143.

Chapter 3

1. Joseph Bayly, *Winterflight* (Waco, TX: Word Books, 1981), pp. 7-10, 40.
2. John Sherrill, *Mother's Song* (Lincoln, NE: Chosen Books, 1982), p. 32. One time rights United States and Canada. English language only.
3. Ibid., pp. 86-95.
4. Derek Humphrey, *Let Me Die Before I Wake* (Los Angeles: Hemlock Society, 1984), p. 1. Used by permission.
5. Ibid., p. 2.
6. Ibid., p. 3.
7. Ibid., p. 6.
8. Ibid., p. 7.
9. Ibid., p. 132.
10. John Jefferson Davis, "Book Review," *Eternity* (January 1987), p. 34.
11. Judie Brown, "There's no dignity in pulling the plug," *USA Today* (October 6, 1986), p. 12A.

Chapter 4

1. Alan L. Otten, "Can't We Put My Mother to Sleep?" *Wall Street Journal* (June 5, 1985), p. 34.
2. Nancy Dickey, "AMA's Statement on withdrawing treatment," *USA Today* (April 2, 1986), p. 9A.

Chapter 5

1. Dennis McLellan, "Nun Asks Open Forum in Life-Support Cases," *Los Angeles Times* (October 13, 1985), p. 16.
2. Bertram and Elsie Bandham, "Rights, Justice and Euthanasia," *Beneficent Euthanasia,* Marvin Kohl, ed. (Buffalo: Prometheus Books, 1975), p. 83. Used by permission.
3. Arthur Dyck, "An Alternative to the Ethic of Euthanasia," *To Live and Die: When, Why, and How,* Robert H. Williams, ed. (New York: Springer-Verlag, 1937), pp. 99-103, 107.
4. H. Richard Neibuhr, quoted on pp. 109-110 in above work.
5. Jerry B. Wilson, *Death by Decision* (Philadelphia: The Westminster Press, 1975), pp. 89-90.
6. Marvin Kohl, "Voluntary Beneficent Euthanasia," *Beneficent Euthanasia,* pp. 131, 134, 135, 139. Used by permission.
7. Ibid. Footnote, *Young India,* Nov. 18, 1926, quoted in *The Essential Gandhi,* Louis Fischer, ed. (New York: Vintage Books, 1962), p. 216.
8. Madeline L'Engle, *The Summer of the Great-Grandmother* (New York: Seabury Press and Harper & Row, Publishers, Inc., 1979), pp. 149-50.

Chapter 6
1. Roger Lincoln Shinn, *Life, Death and Destiny* (Philadelphia: The Westminster Press, 1957), pp. 79, 25, 39.
2. Daniel Hoffman Martin, *Concerning Them That Are Asleep* (Philadelphia: The Westminster Press, 1917), pp. 11-12.
3. Joseph Fletcher, "The 'Right' to Live and the 'Right' to Die," *Beneficent Euthanasia,* Marvin Kohl, ed. (Buffalo, Prometheus Books, 1975), pp. 44-46. Used by permission.
4. Francis A. Schaeffer and C. Everett Koop, *Whatever Happened to the Human Race* (Westchester, IL (60153): Good News Publishers/Crossway Books, 1979), p. 16. Used by permission.
5. Ibid., p. 20.
6. Ibid., p. 117.
7. Howard Clark Kee, *Making Ethical Decisions* (Philadelphia: The Westminster Press, 1957), pp. 12-13.
8. Ibid., pp. 16-17.
9. Ibid., p. 17.

Chapter 7
1. Madeline L'Engle, *The Summer of the Great-Grandmother* (New York: Seabury Press and Harper & Row Publishers, Inc., 1979), p. 40.
2. Florine DuFresne, *Home Care* (Elgin: The Brethren Press, 1983), p. 15. Used by permission.
3. L'Engle, *Summer,* p. 68.
4. "Hospice Program," a St. Joseph Hospital Home Health Network Program brochure.
5. Francis A. Schaeffer and C.Everett Koop, *Whatever Happened to the Human Race?* (Westchester, IL (60153): Good News Publishers/Crossway Books, 1979), p. 116. Used by permission.
6. Saint Joseph Hospital, *Hospice Volunteer Voices,* pp. 2-3.
7. Lois Lemieux, "Jarrod, Strong and Free," *Guideposts* (January 1986), pp. 10-13.

Chapter 8
1. Quoted by Ellen Severoni in an interview for "A Community Health-Care Debate," *Los Angeles Times* (July 14, 1985).
2. Nancy Badgwell, "The Hardest Decision," *Modern Maturity* (December 1986-January 1987), p. 82. Used by author's permission.
3. Ibid., pp. 83-84.
4. Ibid., p. 84.
5. Francis A. Schaeffer and C. Everett Koop, *Whatever Happened to the Human Race?* (Westchester, IL (60153): Good News Publishers/Crossway Books, 1979), p. 117. Used by permission.
6. Jack Silvey Miller, *The Healing Power of Grief* (New York: Seabury Press and Harper & Row Publishers, Inc., 1978), p. xii.
7. Ibid., pp. 3-4.
8. Ibid., pp. 13-15.

Chapter 10
1. William F. Schulz, "Goal is human dignity, not mere spark of 'life,' " *USA Today* (October 6, 1986), p. 12A.
2. Kathryn Ann Lyndskoog, *C. S. Lewis, Mere Christian* (Wheaton, IL: Harold Shaw Publishers, 1987), p. 69
3. Ibid.

4. President's Commission for the Study of Ethical Problems in Medicine and Biomedical and Behavioral Research, *Deciding to Forego Life-Sustaining Treatment* (New York: Concern for Dying, 1983), pp. 3, 5, 50, 88, 89.

Chapter 11
1. Nellie Pike Randall, "My Father's Best Gift," *Reader's Digest* (January 1987), pp. 11-16. Used by permission.
2. Anette Winter, "The Shame of Elder Abuse," *Modern Maturity* (October-November 1986), pp. 50-53. Used with permission from *Modern Maturity*, ©1987, American Association of Retired Persons.
3. Mary C. Senander, *Living Wills* (Minneapolis: Human Life Alliance of Minnesota, Inc.)
4. Gary E. McCueb and Theresa Boucher, *Terminating Life* (Hudson: Gary E. McCueb Publications, Inc., 1985), p. 23.
5. Judie Brown, "There's no dignity in pulling the plug," *USA Today* (October 6, 1986), p. 12A.
6. President's Commission for the Study of Ethical Problems in Medicine and Biomedical and Behavioral Research, *Deciding to Forego Life-Sustaining Treatment* (New York: Concern for Dying, 1983), pp. 95-100, 253, 242-43.
7. Peter Gott, "Hospitalization certification may not be best for patient," *Orange County Register (February 19, 1986), p. E6.*

Chapter 12
1. Dale V. Hardt, *Death: The Final Frontier* (Englewood Cliffs, NJ: Prentice-Hall, 1979), p. 63.
2. Bill Bright, *Witnessing Without Fear* (San Bernardino, CA: Here's Life Publishers, 1987), p. 35.

Chapter 13
1. Madeline L'Engle, *The Summer of the Great-Grandmother* (New York: Seabury Press and Harper & Row, Publishers, Inc., 1979), pp. 227-8.
2. Ibid., p. 243.
3. *The Christian Answer* (New York: Division of Evangelism, Board of National Missions), pp. 14-15.
4. Robert H. Williams, *To Live and Die: When, Why, and How* (New York: Springer-Verlag, 1937), Prologue, p. 1.
5. Daniel Hoffman Martin, *Concerning Them That Are Asleep* (Philadelphia: The Westminster Press, 1917), p. 26.
6. Harold S.Kushner, *When All You've Ever Wanted Isn't Enough* (New York: Summit Books, 1986), p. 156.

Epilogue
1. Chuck Bowden, "Watching death become a reality," *USA Today* (October 6, 1986), p. 12A.

More
Life-Changing
Books

From  **Here's Life Publishers**

FATHER TO SON:
BECOMING A MAN OF HONOR

Merrill J. Oster

A fourth-generation farmboy turned communications company president shares timeless insights with his son on being a man of God in everything from handling finances to choosing a life partner.
0-89840-192-5/$6.95

MOTHER TO DAUGHTER:
BECOMING A WOMAN OF HONOR

Marilyn Willett Heavilin

The author of *Roses in December,* a former high school counselor, draws on experiences as a wife, mother and popular speaker as she explains how to be a woman of God in today's world.
0-89840-193-3/$6.95

"GOD IS NOT FAIR"

Joel A. Freeman

How to come to terms with life's "raw deals." Sensitive, straightforward help from a pastor and licensed counselor.
0-89840-189-5/$5.95

THE HIDDEN STRENGTH

Ingrid Trobisch

The wife of the popular late author Walter Trobisch shows how a deep commitment to the Lord can help you weather the storms of life.
0-89840-200-X/$6.95

BUILDING A RELATIONSHIP THAT LASTS

Dick Purnell

A popular speaker at young adult seminars helps singles find the glue that cements relationships in order to avoid on-again, off-again relationship cycles. Part of the Dynamic Relationships Series. 0-89840-206-9/$6.95

WHAT CAN A MOTHER DO?

FINDING SIGNIFICANCE AT HOME AND BEYOND

Judy Downs Douglass

The author shares how she and dozens of other women have learned to achieve personal significance through a successful balance of mothering and ministry. For mothers of all ages. 0-89840-201-8/$6.95

**Available at your Christian bookstore.
Or call Here's Life Publishers:
1-800-864-5659
In California call (714) 886-7981 collect**

Worldwide Challenge *magazine helps you reach your world for Christ…*

* through insights from Christian leaders and authors like Elisabeth Elliot, Bill Bright, Chuck Colson, Kay Arthur, Chuck Swindoll and others;

* through articles about people like you–home makers, businessmen, mothers, executives, professionals, singles--who are being used of God in extraordinary ways;

* through ideas about how to host a Jesus birthday party for children, how to take a stand for righteousness and how to tell your co-workers about Christ;

* through stories of Campus Crusade for Christ ministries around the world, imparting a vision to you for the world and giving you ideas on how to pray for those missionaries and new believers.

■ *Special Introductory Offer!*

Order your subscription to Worldwide Challenge *magazine at the special introductory price of $7.95 per year. That's $2.00 off the normal $9.95 rate.*

Name_____

Address _____

City_____ State_____ Zip_____

I wish to pay by: ❑ *Check* ❑ *Mastercard* ❑ *Visa*

Card No._____ Expires_____

Authorized Signature _____

Mail to: Worldwide Challenge magazine, Subscriptions
Coordinator, P.O. Box 6710, San Bernardino, CA 92412